Roman Britain

Roman Britain, first published in 1972, gives the young reader a vivid impression of the British Isles immediately preceding, during and after the Roman occupation, which lasted for 400 years. Using a selection of extracts, both historical and imaginative, it offer a suitably comprehensive account of Roman Britain: the campaigns fought to subdue it, the military and civil government established to govern it, relations between the Imperial administration and the natives, and the departure of the legions to fight elsewhere in the Empire.

Selections of poetry by John Masefield, W.H. Auden, Rudyard Kipling and A.E. Housman are included, together with prose extracts from Bede, Tacitus, Hilaire Belloc, Henry Treece, Alfred Duggan and Rudyard Kipling. Physically compact, *Roman Britain* encourages young classicists and historians to engage imaginatively with the subject, which also supplying ample opportunity for more detailed discussion and further reading.

Roman Britain

Edited by

Edward H. Jones
Beryl Jones &
Michael Hayhoe

Routledge
Taylor & Francis Group

First published in 1972
by Routledge & Kegan Paul Ltd

This edition first published in 2014 by Routledge
2 Park Square, Milton Park, Abingdon, Oxon, OX14 4RN
and by Routledge
711 Third Avenue, New York, NY 10017

Routledge is an imprint of the Taylor & Francis Group, an informa business

Publisher's Note
The publisher has gone to great lengths to ensure the quality of this reprint but
points out that some imperfections in the original copies may be apparent.

Disclaimer
The publisher has made every effort to trace copyright holders and welcomes
correspondence from those they have been unable to contact.

ISBN 13: 978-1-138-02157-0 (hbk)
ISBN 13: 978-1-315-77767-2 (ebk)
ISBN 13: 978-1-138-02159-4 (pbk)

Themes

Roman Britain

London: Routledge & Kegan Paul

First published 1972
by Routledge & Kegan Paul Ltd
Broadway House, 68–74 Carter Lane,
London EC4V 5EL
Printed in Great Britain by
Alden & Mowbray Ltd
at the Alden Press, Oxford

ISBN 0 7100 7160 4 (c)
ISBN 0 7100 7161 2 (p)

Contents

The long peace

The Romans leave

Note

When verse or prose is quoted from a work, the title of the original source is given at the end of the passage; when no source is given, the passage is complete in itself and appears with its original title.

Acknowledgments

We should like to express our thanks for permission to use the following works, or extracts from them:
Tacitus: *On Britain and Germany*, transl. H. Mattingly (Penguin Books Ltd); Bede: *A History of the English Church and People*, transl. Leo Sherley-Price (Penguin Books Ltd); Charles Williams: 'Caesar at the straits' (the author's executors and the Clarendon Press, Oxford); Hilaire Belloc: *The Eye-Witness* (A. D. Peters & Company); Wilfrid Gibson: *I Heard a Sailor* (Mr Michael Gibson and Macmillan & Co. Ltd); Henry Treece: *Legions of the Eagle* (The Bodley Head); two extracts from *The Queen's Brooch* (Hamish Hamilton Ltd); Cecil Roberts: *Selected Poems* (Hutchinson & Co. Ltd); Ian Serraillier: *Miscellany Six* (Oxford University Press); John James: *Not for all the Gold in Ireland* (Cassell & Co. Ltd); G. M. Durant: *Britain, Rome's Most Northerly Province* (G. Bell & Sons Ltd); Henry Treece: 'Song of the Ninth (Hispana) Legion' from *Red Queen, White Queen* (The Bodley Head); Stephanie Plowman: *To Spare the Conquered* (Associated Book Publishers Ltd); John Masefield: *Collected Poems* (the Society of Authors as the literary representative of the Estate of John Masefield); W. H. Barrett: *Tales from the Fens* (Routledge & Kegan Paul Ltd); Andrew Young: *Collected Poems 1960* (Rupert Hart-Davies Ltd); Rudyard Kipling: *Puck of Pook's Hill* (Mrs George Bambridge and Macmillan & Co. Ltd); W. H. Auden: 'Roman Wall Blues' from *Collected Shorter Poems 1927–1957* (Faber & Faber Ltd); Alfred Duggan: two extracts from *The Little Emperors* (Faber & Faber Ltd); D. R. Barker: *The Story of Roman Britain* (Edward Arnold Ltd); George Shipway: *Imperial Governor* (Peter Davies Ltd, 1968); Rosemary Sutcliff: *The Lantern Bearers* (Oxford University Press); A. E. Housman: *Collected Poems* (the Society of Authors as the literary representative of the Estate of A. E. Housman, and Jonathan Cape Ltd, publishers of A. E. Housman's *Collected Poems*).

CORNOVII

LUGI

SMERTAE

DECANTAE

CALEDONES

CREONES

EBUDII

TAEZALI

VACOMAGI

Pinnata Castra
INCHTUTHIL

Horrea Classis
CARPOW

VENICONES

Antonine Wall

DAMNONII

Credigona
CARRIDEN

VOTADINI

Trimontium
NEWSTEAD

SELGOVAE

Vercovicium
HOUSESTEADS

Pons Aelius
NEWCASTLE

Arbeia
SOUTH SHIELDS

NOVANTAE

Luguvalium
CARLISLE

Hadrian's Wall

Glannaventa
RAVENGLASS

MONAVIA
Isle of Man

Cataractonium
CATTERICK

BRIGANTES

Olicana
ILKLEY

Eboracum
YORK

PARISI

Petuaria
BROUGH

Mamucium
MANCHESTER

Danum
DONCASTER

MONA
Anglesey

Segontium
CAERNARVON

Deva
CHESTER

DECEANGLI

Lindum
LINCOLN

CORNOVII

CORITANI

ERMINE STREET

Viroconium
WROXETER

Ratae
LEICESTER

ICENI

Venta Icenorum
CAISTOR

ORDOVICES

Salinae
DROITWICH

Magnis
KENCHESTER

WATLING STREET

FOSSE WAY

Durolipons
CAMBRIDGE

Moridunum
CARMARTHEN

DEMETAE

SILURES

DOBUNNI

Glevum
GLOUCESTER

CATUVELLAUNI

TRINOVANTES

Camulodunum
COLCHESTER

Isca Silurum
CAERLEON

Venta Silurum
CAERWENT

Corinium
CIRENCESTER

Verulamium
ST ALBANS

Londinium
LONDON

Aquae Sulis
BATH

ATREBATES

Pontes
STAINES

Calleva Atrebatum
SILCHESTER

Durovernum
CANTERBURY

Rutupiae
RICHBOROUGH

BELGAE

Venta Belgarum
WINCHESTER

CANTIACI

Dubris
DOVER

Lindinis
ILCHESTER

Sorviodunum
OLD SARUM

REGNENSES

DUROTRIGES

Isca
Dumnoniorum
EXETER

Durnovaria
DORCHESTER

Novomagus
CHICHESTER

DUMNONII

VECTIS

Deva	Roman name
CHESTER	Modern English name
ICENI	British tribe
⊙	Towns
✱	Coloniae (Settlements of retired legionaries)
✗	Legionary fortresses
●	Forts
——	Roads in *The Antonine Itinerary* - a 3rd century Road Book - of routes used by Imperial officials
- - -	Other roads

The fair land

1   A Roman's view of Britain

P. CORNELIUS TACITUS

What was Roman Britain like?

The Romans occupied this northernmost province of their Empire for some 400 years. In the first two brief passages, we see different attitudes towards the land. The first is by Tacitus from his life of Agricola, a famous general of the early Roman occupation and a governor of Britain. He assesses the value of Britain as a province of Rome.

Britain, the largest of the islands known to us Romans, is so shaped and situated as to face Germany on the East and Spain on the West, while to the South it actually lies in full view of Gaul. Its northern shores, with no land confronting them, are beaten by a wild and open sea. . . .

The climate is objectionable, with its frequent rains and mists, but there is no extreme cold. Their day is longer than is normal in the Roman world. The night is bright and, in the extreme North, short, with only a brief interval between evening and morning twilight. If no clouds block the view, the sun's glow, it is said, can be seen all night long. It does not set and rise, but simply passes along the horizon. The reason must be that the ends of the earth, being flat, cast low shadows and cannot raise the darkness to any height; night therefore fails to reach the sky and its stars. The soil can bear all produce, except the olive, the vine, and other natives of warmer climes, and it is fertile. Crops are slow to ripen, but quick to grow— both facts due to one and the same cause, the extreme moistness of land and sky. Britain yields gold, silver and other metals, to make it worth conquering. Ocean, too, has its pearls, but they are dusky and mottled. Some think that the natives are unskilful in gathering them. Whereas in the Red Sea the oysters are torn alive and breathing

3

from the rocks, in Britain they are collected as the sea throws them up. I find it easier to believe in a defect of quality in the pearls than of greed in us.

From *Agricola* transl. H. Mattingly

2 Britain (AD 731)

BEDE

In this second passage, written by a learned English monk called Bede some 300 years after the Romans had left Britain, the author writes as a lover of his native land.

Britain is rich in grain and timber; it has good pasturage for cattle and draught animals, and vines are cultivated in various localities. There are many land and sea birds of various species, and it is well known for its plentiful springs and rivers abounding in fish. Salmon and eels are especially plentiful, while seals, dolphins, and sometimes whales are caught. There are also many varieties of shell-fish, such as mussels, in which are found excellent pearls of several colours, red, purple, violet, and green, but mainly white. Whelks are abundant, and a beautiful scarlet dye is extracted from them which remains unfaded by sunshine or rain; indeed, the older the cloth, the more beautiful its colour. The country has both salt springs and hot springs, and the waters flowing from them provide hot baths, in which the people bathe separately according to age and sex. As Saint Basil says: 'Water receives heat when it flows across certain metals, and becomes hot, and even scalding.' The land has rich veins of many metals, including copper, iron, lead, and silver. There is also much jet of fine quality, a black jewel which can be set on fire and, when burned, drives away snakes and, like amber, when it is warmed by friction, it holds fast whatever is applied to it. In old times, the country had twenty-eight noble cities, besides innumerable strongholds, which also were guarded by walls, towers, and barred gates

Since Britain lies far north toward the pole, the nights are short in summer, and at midnight it is hard to tell whether the evening twilight still lingers or whether dawn is approaching, since the sun at night passes not far below the earth in its journey round the north back to the east. Consequently the days are long in summer, as are the nights in winter when the sun withdraws into African regions, as long in fact as eighteen hours, whereas the summer nights and winter days are very short, and last only six hours.

From *A History of the English Church and People*
transl. L. Sherley-Price

3 Britannia

Britain was thought to be on the edge of the world, and the poem
which follows shows the Romans' pride in conquering their most
northerly province. It commemorates the invasion of Britain by the
Emperor Claudius in AD 43–7, whose legions were commanded by
the great general Aulus Plautius.

Semota et vasto disiuncta Britannia ponto,
cinctaque inaccessis horrida litoribus,
quam pater invictis Nereus velaverat undis,
quam fallax aestu circuit Oceanus,
brumalem sortita polum, qua frigida semper
praefulget stellis Arctos inocciduis,
conspectu devicta tuo, Germanice Caesar,
subdidit insueto colla premenda iugo.
aspice, confundat populos ut pervia tellus;
coniunctum est, quod adhuc orbis et orbis erat.

Britain, by the immeasurable sea stranded,
Remote, barbaric, beset by unapproachable shores;
Which the father of the Nereids concealed with invincible
    waves,
And the treacherous ocean encircles with seething tides;
A cold land, chance recipient of the wintry sky
Where the constellations glitter with unsetting stars:
Subdued utterly at your approach, Germanicus Caesar,
She bent her neck to the weight of an unfamiliar yoke.
See, the known lands mingle their peoples;
Two worlds are now united, that were once apart.

Translated by Rachel Woodrow

Invasion

4 Caesar at the straits

CHARLES WILLIAMS

It was in 55 BC that the Roman army, under the command of Julius Caesar, made its first foray to the shores of Britain. This poem imagines what was in Caesar's mind as he assembled his troops.

Caesar stood on the ramparts
 of the farthest Roman wall,
with the camps and marches behind him
 that meant a conquered Gaul;
and wide before him a ghostly sea:
saying: 'And what may Britain be?'

Caesar stood on the ramparts,
 hearing how boatmen hear
the calling ghosts at midnight
 and rise in haste and fear
those travellers o'er the straits to row;
saying: 'Where the ghosts go Rome may go!'

Caesar stood on the ramparts
 and saw across the wave
how the storms come in winter
 but seamanship may save;
keeping a gallant mind within,
saying: 'What of the soldiers' discipline?'

Caesar stood on the ramparts,
 and looked o'er the curving foam,
with the stout centurions by him,
and the eagles and ranks of Rome:
saying: 'Bid the ships do thus and thus',
and the world of Caesar came to us.

5   The two soldiers

HILAIRE BELLOC

On 26 August 55 BC, Julius Caesar sailed from Boulogne with two legions for the invasion of Britain.

Caesar was the general, but it was his men who did the fighting. This short story by Hilaire Belloc describes two soldiers of one of the legions of the army as they sailed across the Channel to the island.

The night was very warm in Picardy, for August was not yet done, and the heated air of the day still quivered over the bare stubble of the hillsides upon either side of the great landlocked harbour, when that famous regiment, the Tenth, the greatest of the Roman Legions, stood formed along the quay; along that quay lay for a mile and more, all the way from Pont-de-Briques northwards, a great mass of transports with their gangways fixed and everything ready for going aboard. The waning quarter-moon shone fully upon the ranks of men, rising beyond that main hill to the east which hid the plains beyond. It was not yet midnight.

As the men stood at ease in the ranks talking to each other in low tones, a non-commissioned officer came rapidly down the water front, glancing with quick eyes to note, where the lanterns shone on them, the numbers of the companies; for these were marked in rough white figures upon little boards which stood in the ground. Then when he had found what he wanted he approached his comrade in command and communicated an order. That comrade turned and called out in Latin two names, whereat two men, certainly not Roman, and men whose true names were very different from their regimental sound, stepped out quickly and stood together. They were the artificers of their section, and were drafted for the catapults upon the faster ships, the galleys that lay towards the mouth of the harbour. The one man, who was short, very broad-shouldered, bullet headed, vivacious and young, had for his name Kerdoc; the other, who was tall, softer in the flesh, with heavy limbs, and pale, rather uncertain blue eyes, was called Chlothar; the first was from Beauce, from the edge of that plain, half a day's march or more beyond Chartres and the upper waters of the Eure, the second from the eastern slopes of the Vosges, where a cosy little wooden village had nourished his boyhood, high up on the mountain side from whence could be seen far off the forests of the Allmen.

Many other artificers so selected were drafted in until a column of perhaps a hundred had been formed, then they marched them up the long wharf of wooden piles, got them aboard the first fast galley, bade them ship the gangway, and at last left them free as the sailors; some of them cast off, some of them ran to stand at the halyards.

The moon was high when all these preparations were accomplished, but the air was still very warm, the stars showed but thinly through the summer haze; from the south-west right up the valley of the harbour towards the sea blew a faint but steady breeze. The galleys weighed, and with very gentle and rhythmical strokes of the oars they dropped in file down the sluggish ebb of the neap tide till they came to the narrow mouth of this great port of Icht and took the open sea.

Kerdoc and Chlothar, the elder and the younger, the short man and the tall, the dark man and the fair, leant over the bulwark of the weather side and watched, with some fear but with a great exhilaration, this new element the sea.

Slight as the wind was, there was not a little jump upon the bar of the Liane, and each of them had a qualm of sickness, but very soon, when they were well out of the narrows, the galley was put before the wind and the steady run of the vessel eased them. All that they heard and saw filled them with life: the new noise of the water alongside, the creaking of the cordage, the high sing-song cries of the sailors when an order was given to haul, and the even beat of the oars; as also, above them, an infinite expanse of sky; before them, as it seemed, an infinite expanse of water in the dusk of the night. In one place they could see over their shoulders the indistinct mass of Grisnez rising above the coast and blotting out the few horizon stars; upon all the rest of the ring around them, from the extreme south-west to the east, there was nothing but a hazy line where the dark sea mingled with the night sky. Very soon the motion of the ship seemed to change, the sea grew easier, the wind was steady, and the bows took the water with a longer sweep, because the tide had turned and was now running slowly eastward up the Straits. In an hour it began to be light.

First, the little seas showed fresh and grey under the beginnings of dawn, the colours slowly grew both upon the water and upon the ships around; at last could be made out like a picture the whole sweep of the Gallic shore, for they had gone but few miles under the light air and against the ebb during the last hours of darkness.

With the flood tide, however, and the breeze still holding they made more rapidly out toward mid-Channel, and when the sun sprang up above the eastern edge of the world they could clearly see before them the new shore which they had hitherto but dimly perceived on specially clear days from the heights of the camp above Boulogne. It was a long, low line of dirty white, as yet miles and miles away, and sinking at either end into a flat that did not show above the sea. With the exhilaration of the daylight the conversation of the two men grew animated and full. They conversed in the Pidgin Latin of the regiment, the one with the sharp hammered accents and thin vowels of the Gaul, the other with the slurred gutturals of the German.

And first they talked of the miseries and misfortune of the service, and agreed upon their bad luck that they should have been picked out of their regiment (a hard enough service, God knows!) to herd with common barbarians, who were not soldiers but mechanics, for each had (though it was not the form of the army to show it) a swelling pride in the Tenth, and, indeed, it was a famous regiment. . . .

Next, then, as the morning grew and the sun of August rose, throwing long shadows of ships athwart the sea, they talked of the danger of such voyages; talking bombastically like landsmen, and thinking that in this calm night they had come through perils.

'But I cannot drown,' said Kerdoc wisely, wagging his head. 'I have a charm against water, and I cannot die by it.'

'Show me your charm,' said Chlothar, a little sulkily, for he was jealous of so much power.

Kerdoc hesitated somewhat: it was a great confidence; then he remembered how long Chlothar and he had marched side by side—nearly a year altogether—and he furtively pulled a little bronze medal from his neck, where it hung by a chain, and showed it in the palm of his hand to his comrade. There was a crescent moon stamped upon it, with a star on either tip, and in the curve of the crescent the face of a goddess.

Chlothar looked at it with horror. He thrust out the fore and little fingers of his right hand, clenching the others, and put his hand out over the sea, making the sign of the Horned God who protected him from the influence of the Moon; then he said in a slow, but angry, manner: 'Put it away; I will not look at a figure of the Moon. He is evil!'

Kerdoc was stung in his quick nature by the insult, but proud in his vanity at the effect and power of his charm; his vanity conquered and he said with a somewhat ridiculous swagger: 'The priests gave it me; or rather,' he added slyly, 'they gave it me as against a rich offering. I got it in the Grotto where they sacrifice to the Virgin who shall bear a Son.'

The German knew that famous place, and could not avoid an expression of respect. Kerdoc quickly took advantage of that mood to exalt himself.

'That Grotto,' he said, 'is within the limits of my tribe; my mother had a cousin who was priest there underground.'

Chlothar said nothing, but looked sullen for some time, and then said brutally: 'Time may come and the army will do hurt to your village!' It was a common taunt in the regiment against all newly enlisted men, and Kerdoc let it pass by, but he was still sore when he remembered the gesture the German had made to his Goddess, and for some time there was silence between them, and both men looked over the side.

They were now, however, close under the British shore, and the activity of the men about them, sailors shifting ropes, tautening sheets, or running forward with bare feet to execute a command, showed them that change had come upon their journey. The wind had dropped, a long smooth swell had taken the place of the small choppy waves, the water was already slack and just upon the ebb again, when—to one command which the trumpets sounded down the line of galleys—the anchors were dropped and the boats swung round east and west, head to stream, all in rank under the chalk walls of Britain.

Upon the skyline along the edge of the cliffs, hiding the burnt summer turf with their multitude, were thousands upon thousands of the islanders.

15

They kept but little order; at every few yards along the mass a taller figure showed upon the platform of a chariot, the whole host was moving and seething like a column of ants, and even at that distance could be heard from time to time over the carrying surface of the water a whirl of distant cheers, or more clearly the braying of short conches blown loudly and discordantly in random defiance. Now and again some one of them would hurl his spear over the edge of the cliff till it fell upon the chalk at the base, or, by some exceptional feat, just pass the tide-line of the sea, and caught the surf where the swell of the high tide broke against the shore.

All this the two soldiers of the Tenth watched curiously. Chlothar said: 'I wonder how they come on!' To him, as to all private soldiers, the indolent prospect of approaching action (however insignificant the action promised to be) was unpleasing.

Kerdoc assumed a different mood. 'I can tell you,' he said, affecting an experience which his youth did not possess, 'they are Gwentish men; I have heard them called Gwentish men. Now men of the Gwent fight by rushes, and are easily broken. We have some such to the north of us at home. They cannot break a line; it is all looks and shouting. My father has fought against Gwentish men,' he added apologetically, seeing a look of bovine doubt in Chlothar's eye, and recognizing that his criticism of the fighting had been vague; 'I do not say that I have, but my father has. Sometimes the men of our village would fight them in a band, and sometimes two by two for a prize.'

.   .   .   .   .   .

The sun rose to his meridian and declined, the fleet still lay upon the oily sea under the heat at anchor, when toward mid-afternoon the breeze rose again, and as it rose the galleys slowly swung round, bringing their sterns from west to east as the tide returned. With that moment was perceived, after so many hours, the group of the heavy transports bowling up from the south-west with the wind and the sea together, but of the cavalry that should have appeared to the left of that fleet in the little ships from Ambleteuse there was not a sign.

A pinnace set out from a central galley to meet the newcomers with orders, and on the deck of that galley stood the great awning of Tyrian cloth which covered Caesar.

From *The Eye-Witness*

16

6 First landing

G. F. SCOTT ELLIOT

This highly coloured account of Caesar's invasion was written over half a century ago. It is a typical example of the rather romantic way of presenting history in schools at that time.

It was at midnight on the 25th August, B.C. 55, that what is now Boulogne had witnessed the departure of the first Roman invasion. There were no less than eighty transport ships, carrying the two famous legions (7th and 10th), in which Caesar placed his trust. There were many long galleys, also crowded with the best slingers, archers, and artillery men that the Roman world could produce. The cavalry (500 Gaulish horsemen) had gone to embark at Ambleteuse, a few miles off, but they never reached Britain, being delayed by unfavourable weather.

It was about seven on the next morning that the British army council at their camp, near Canterbury, were roused by mounted messengers with the news that the Roman fleet was in sight. About nine in the morning they were all on Shakespeare's cliff, near Dover, and witnessed the approach of the Roman galleys.

The British forces were collecting hurriedly all day long, and great quantities of flints, stones, and lumps of rock were prepared at the edge of the cliffs, to hurl over and destroy any rash invader who dared to set his foot on the English shore.

The galleys, however, rolled peacefully at anchor, waiting for the great ships, which did not arrive until three or four in the afternoon. Why this delay? What were they about to do? But at five o'clock they hauled up their cables, and with wind and tide in their favour turned eastward and ran up channel. Then every horse's head was turned to the east, and the rattling, leaping war-chariots and cavalry of the British raced one another over the short turf and undulating downs

17

past St. Margaret's and Kingsdown, and on towards Walmer Castle.

They had left the Downs, and arrived at a small rising hill (near where Walmer Castle now lies sheltered in its woodlands), when the Roman navy stopped; every ship suddenly veered round, and was driven straight and at full speed towards the land.

They grounded on the sloping shingle, and were immovably beached. But the low-lying shore and the beds of shingle were by this time crowded with British warriors.

For some considerable time the Romans soldiers hesitated, for indeed the prospect was anything but attractive. The water was five to six feet deep at the bows of the grounded ships. They knew nothing of the ground except that it was loose shingle, slipping under the feet, and dragged back and forward by the waves. They themselves were heavily armed, and carried great shields, swords, and spears. The Britons were charging through the water. Now a pair of fierce, sturdy little horses dragged a bumping, clattering chariot right into the waves; within it some huge, painted, red-haired chieftain was supporting himself by one hand on the basket work, and roaring with fantastic rage as he brandished a great spear held ready to transfix any stumbling legionary. The noise was overpowering, for every Briton was yelling and shouting; and the discordant blare of innumerable Keltic trumpets never stopped for an instant. The British horses had been trained to the sea, and their riders hovered about ready to surround any soldier that dared to jump into the water. No wonder that the Romans were for some minutes held in check.

But Divus Caesar was upon one of those ships. An order was passed along, and then the long, low, black, and wicked-looking galleys formed in line, and were rowed at full speed straight on to the beach to the left of and close beside the stranded ships. Above their bulwarks appeared the brutal faces of savage Numidian archers and the heads of keen and crafty Cretan bowmen. There were also slingers from Minorca and Ivica, famed for their skill throughout all the Roman world, and, besides these, strange creaking engines made of beams and hides were hurriedly mounted in the prows of the galleys. Then began a pitiless rain of whizzing deadly arrows, of bullets of hardened clay or of lead, and especially of great rough stones and rocks flung by the catapults. This awful storm of deadly projectiles struck full on the left flank of the disordered Britons suddenly and unexpectedly; no horses, however well trained, could withstand it, and

18

many charioteers lost control of their animals, which increased the confusion. So the Britons began to fall back and give way in disorder.

Now was the opportunity of the Romans. A few legionaries dropped into the water, but they still hesitated to go forward. Then with a loud cry the standard-bearer of the 10th called upon his gods to bless the legion and to favour them in their enterprise.

'Spring down, fellow-soldiers, unless you want to shamefully lose your eagle to the enemy. As for me, I will do my duty to the Republic and to my general.'

Then he jumped into the water, and steadily carried the eagle, straight toward the enemy. The soldiers, shouting to each other, hurried after him, but the fortune of the day was not yet decided. The Britons dashed into the water, surrounding and trying to kill the soldiers before they got their footing on land. But then the ships' boats filled with javelin-throwers and archers went to their assistance. In the end certain of the legionaries made good their footing on dry land, and then all the efforts of Cassivellaun and the other chieftains were futile, for fresh bodies of soldiers still disembarked to join them. In vain did the British chiefs encourage their men, and gallop in chariots to wherever the Britons gave way. At last the Roman lieutenant gave a short stern order, and the line of heavy-armed legionaries advanced steadily, driving before it, and maiming or slaying the Britons, who could make no effective resistance.

From *The Romance of Early British Life*

7   The buried camp

Caesar tried again in the following year, 54 BC, but failed. Though his contact with Britain was brief, it is through his name that most people remember the might of Rome.

Fear not: the dead are dead,
And fallen pomp and power
Leave no pale ghosts to prowl
Above their earthly bed:
'Twas no dead Roman but a living owl
That startled us beside the ruined tower.

And yet, that beak, those eyes
That blazed out from the night!
Surely 'twas Caesar's soul
That with sharp stabbing cries
Swept by, as through the buried camp we stole,
Spurring dead cohorts on to one last fight.

From *I Heard a Sailor*

8 Battle in the sun

HENRY TREECE

Almost 100 years went by after Caesar's invasions. Then the Romans came again. On the orders of Emperor Claudius, Aulus Plautius led his legions into Britain in AD 43 to subdue the land and make it part of the Roman Empire for some 350 years.

In this extract from *Legions of the Eagle* by Henry Treece, the son of a British chieftain sees the Romans battle against the British leader Caradoc (or Caratacus, as the Romans called him) outside Camulodunum, the present-day Colchester in Essex.

Under the summer sun that day the fate of a country was to be decided, and the two boys, watching from a hillock over half a mile away from the conflict, gazed with set faces, their hearts beating with excitement. Even Bel was caught up in this frenzied atmosphere and, as trumpets blew from the Roman side and the long war-horns howled from the Celtic side, the small hound leapt on his thong-lead with an excitement as pronounced as that of his young master, whining and scratching the springy turf, as he tried to break away and run from this immense turmoil which now seemed to approach and now retreat from the watchers on the hill. Down there it seemed that half the world had assembled to do battle, for the plain was now dark with a multitude of men.

The Roman cohorts were in position now, the sturdy, loud-voiced centurions and decurions pushing and beating the headstrong legionaries into the formation they required; the noble young officers, with their red horse-hair plumes floating in the breeze and their blue cloaks puffing out behind them like smoke, galloping from company to company, calling out now and again, and pointing here and there with their gilded staffs or long cavalry swords.

The infantry of the Legion was in place, solid and waiting, each

21

man bearing his shield well before his body, his long lance held up and slightly pointed forward, ready for the command to advance.

Then a great hush settled over the tumultuous preparations, for there was a series of blasts on the long silver trumpets, and line after line of Roman archers marched forward, past the waiting ranks of infantrymen, accompanied by cheers as they went, each man with his head held proudly and erect, to take up their positions at the very front of the foremost line, protected only by one rank of shieldsmen.

Gwydion watched them in admiration, as did the various groups of Celtic tribesmen who sat, here and there, facing the Romans, on the broad plain. Gwydion looked over towards his own massed countrymen, and recognized many of the tribes by the colours of their tunics and plaids; Cantii, Trinobantes, his mother's own people, the Atrebates, even certain groups of Iceni, who had always spoken well of Rome in the past; but he noticed that there were no Brigantes, even though their old queen, Cartismandua, had been one of the first to promise help to Caratacus when his great father, Cunobelinus, had died a year or so before.

These tribes were all spearmen and swordsmen and archers. The cavalry were out of sight, behind that high hill which lay over towards the city. So were the chariots, which would be led by the king himself. These would not go into action until the crowding, jostling footmen had had their opportunity of slaughter and plunder, for that was a standing agreement between the battle-leaders of the various tribes.

Then, far from the rear of the Roman multitudes, came riding men in coloured skin tunics, and high sheepskin hats, each one with a feather, and usually a heron's feather, stuck in its point. Gwydion stared at them, at their long horn bows and little shaggy ponies, and he gasped. For now he knew what that man was whom he had seen in the wood that night—a Roman horseman, a wild rider from Scythia, and not a god at all! And as his mind went back, he wondered whether the man he had seen was a spy, or a deserter from Rome, a horseman who was tired of serving a heartless Empire that, at the end of his twenty years of service would offer him little more reward than mere citizenship of Rome. . . . But Gwydion's thoughts were rudely shattered then, for, with a wild skirling of horns and beating of gongs, the Celts opened the attack, moving swiftly down the hill in small vicious groups, like a great cloud shadow on a sunlit day,

22

harrying the enemy at various points and in various ways, some with the spear, some with bows, and some with knives, at close quarters. Yet though the tribes always left heaps of dead, their own and those of Rome, behind them, the formation of the Legions did not falter, and the shield-wall stayed, as solid as before.

Here and there among the widespread tumult the boys saw the tribesmen tearing off their clothes and armour and, singing a wild death song, begin to dash across the stony plain towards the stolid ranks of Rome. Sometimes, as these madmen approached, their enemies cheered them on, and even laughed at them, until they fell, pierced by sword or javelin, a yard or two from the impregnable shield-wall.

This sporadic fighting might have gone on for long enough, with the archers and the shaggy horsemen waiting, smiling superciliously, and the great gold Eagle of the Legion still shining proudly in the afternoon sun; but then something else happened. Suddenly there was a shower of rain, which beat down out of the summer sky without warning, and in the midst of it appeared a great, brightly coloured rainbow that seemed to arch itself immediately over the Celtic tribes. A great whisper rose from the armies, a sound like the hissing waves of the sea on a rocky shore; and the massed tribesmen seemed to shudder as they drew back and fell to their knees, many of them offering thanks to their gods for this omen of victory. Then the shower passed as suddenly as it had begun and the rainbow went with it, leaving the battlefield a place of great stillness and expectation.

Then, before the footmen of the tribes could regain their feet to attack again, there came the high wailing sound of the king's own war-horns, the signal for the chariots, and to the wonder of the boys, there rose above the hill the many-coloured pennants of these carts of death.

'Look, oh look!' said Gwydion aloud. 'The king has come! The king has come, and my father will be close to him in the battle line!'

Then, as the boy had said, foremost in the long line came the ebony and gold chariot of Caratacus, its red dragon flag furling and unfurling as the winds caught it and let it go again. At the king's right hand, and smiling at his master, stood Gwydion's father, Caswallawn, holding the reins lightly and waiting for the signal to charge. Gwydion stared at the family chariot, for it looked so different now, so dangerous and even wicked, though he had played on it, climbing in and out of it in the stables for as long as he could remember, and he had never thought of it as being a cruel weapon of destruction before. Now it thrilled him that his house should be represented, and so near to the king too. He saw the golden-haired Caratacus, with his great horned gold helmet, turn and say something to his father, and the chariots manoeuvred close together so that the two men could shake each other by the hand.

'Did you see that!' said Gwydion in an ecstasy. 'Oh, I wish I could be with them today! Don't you, Math?'

But Math stared, dark-eyed and serious, for he was watching another people, not his own, and he did not see the fine glory of it all, as Gwydion did. He did not answer.

Then the king took the red dragon banner and took it in his hands, and whirled it round his head, once, twice, and on the third sweep flung it high into the air. A gasp of wonder broke from the Roman ranks. Then down came the banner and Caratacus caught it and shouted. And from the throats of all the tribesmen came the great deep shout, 'Caradoc! Caradoc! We are your dogs, who wish to die for you! Caradoc! Caradoc!' Math had time merely to glance at his friend, and to note the tears of glory that stood in his light-blue eyes, and then the chariots began to roll forward, slowly at first, for the charioteers found it difficult to manage their restive horses who knew they were in battle again after many months of idleness in field and barn.

Then, like some monster slowly gathering speed, the chariot line moved, first at a walk, then at a canter, and at last at a gallop; and from the massed cohorts came sharp orders and the sudden screams of the Roman trumpets. In his excitement, Gwydion moved from the shelter of the rock behind which he had been standing, and ran out into the open. Math followed him, himself almost caught up in the magic of the battle. Then came the clash, and for a while there was nothing but a vast maelstrom of shields and spears and charioteers tumbled in the dust.

Gwydion scanned the broken line and saw that his father and the king were safe. Then he looked at the Roman line, but all the spaces had been filled, and it was as though there had been no change. The chariots retired for a while, drawing back a hundred paces, while the footmen went in again, hacking and stabbing and trying to break the first shield-wall. Then they, too, withdrew, leaving many of their comrades behind them, and once again the king waved his red banner; but this time, before the charge could roll forward on its way, a strange thing happened—the shield-wall seemed to melt away, the line of men swinging like a great gate, to right and to left, leaving exposed the archers, each one erect and bearing his bow drawn to its full and directed towards the Celts. There was a sudden call on the horn and a shout from a centurion who controlled the archers, and the air was full of the hum of arrows, as though a great beehive had suddenly been kicked over and the angry swarm had rushed out to avenge the outrage. Charioteers toppled from their platforms, axemen who stood on the central shaft between the horses fell, clutching their throats or their chests; horses snorted and sank to their knees. Then the shield-wall closed again and the archers were hidden.

'A Roman trick,' shouted Gwydion. 'The trick of a wicked people!' But Math did not know what to think; he clasped his friend's hand tightly, and looked to see that Caswallawn was still safe, still beside his king.

So the chariots moved again, those that were left, and once again the shield-wall took them, swaying a little, breaking here and there, but never collapsing. This time, before the chariots might withdraw again, the final stage of the drama was enacted. The Roman commander had sized up the Celtic method of attack, and now acted as he thought fit. There was a long thin scream on the trumpet, and from either side of the cohorts came the galloping of hooves and the high wild shouting of the little Scythians, their sheepskin hats bobbing in the wind, their bows ready bent, their barbed arrows already flying into the whirling mass of the disorganized chariots. Gwydion saw his father go down, and watched the Romans run forward to him, thrusting with their javelins again and again, as the Scythians swept round and round, shooting as the desire took them now, at all fugitives. Math saw the king's chariot swing round, the red banner trailing tattered behind it, and gallop fast towards the brow of the hill. A few Scythian horsemen tried to follow it, but they were dragged from their ponies by equally savage tribesmen who formed a rearguard after their defeated master. Then Math heard Gwydion give a great sob and a shout, and saw that he was running down towards the thick of the battle. He did the only thing a friend could do, and followed him, Bel now running free at his side, his thong-lead dragging behind him.

Gwydion found himself running, almost as though in a dream,

hardly realizing that his feet were touching the hard ground. The chaos of battle seemed to involve him, many strange sounds buffeted his ears, the shouts of men, the neighing of horses, the screaming of many trumpets. Then he saw the great siege engines looming over him as he ran into the thick of the surging masses—the giant catapults and slings, the grim and ornamented battering-rams that would never need to be used now. He skirted their threatening shapes and found himself among men, men groaning and swearing and praying to their many gods, and was carried hither and thither like a frail cork in a turbulent stream. He saw swords and lances moving about him, and banners floating over his head, but he did not once stop to think that he might be putting himself in danger; all that was in his mind now was to go to his father, whom he had seen tumble from the chariot, already limp, his head thrown back, his helmet falling off.

Once the surging sway of the conflict carried him towards the great heap of war-carts that had crashed into each other when those fearful arrows had taken their toll. He even recognized their own chariot as he moved past it as in a nightmare; he thought he saw his father lying across a broken wheel, his broad chest pierced in many places with red-hackled shafts. Then his eyes misted over, and had he not been swept along by the mixed crowd of Cantii and Romans, stabbing and cutting at each other desperately, he must surely have fallen in a faint on the ground. Then, amidst all this clamour and confusion, his benumbed senses were aware of a new sound, a strange urgent trumpeting, a cross between a roar of anger and a shrill cry of agony. It was a sound that he had never heard, or hoped to hear, before. Then the men about him seemed to scatter, to fade like a morning mist before the first gusts of day. A great space was cleared about him, for the men had fled, and now he saw this new horror which had cut through them like a deadly scythe. A long line of fantastic beasts was thundering down upon the remnants of the Celtic forces; great hunched beasts, with trunks and tusks, and armoured headgear, from the centre of which long murderous spikes projected, to pierce all who could not make their escape, Celt or Roman, it did not matter which. And on the shoulders of each of these beasts sat a negro, dressed in coloured finery, grinning and shouting hoarsely, encouraging the elephants which had never before been used in battle on the soil of Britain.

Gwydion stopped in his headlong rush, staggered as the beasts

26

rumbled towards him, tried to run before them for a pace or two, and then from fear and exhaustion, slipped and fell to the trampled earth.

So he lay, half-unconscious in terror, while the ground about him shuddered with the impact of those immense feet. He did not dare to wonder whether he would live or die; he only lay still, and sobbed on the dusty soil, all the fight gone out of him; and at last something struck him on the head and in the middle of the back, and he knew no more.

From *Legions of the Eagle*

Following on

1 Write an account of how two native warriors journey to the coast to meet the Roman invaders. Describe their first sight of the invaders, their comments and thoughts, and the early stages of the battle which follows.

2 Describe in detail one incident from the battle, as though you were Chlothar in 'The two soldiers'. Perhaps it would be an incident in which Kerdoc's easy confidence would be shaken.

3 Write a letter home to your family in Rome, describing the sea-journey to Britain and your first taste of battle. Perhaps you would have seen captured prisoners, in which case describe them, as well as your first night spent ashore in Britain.

4 Imagine the scene on the day after the battle. Write an account, in the same imaginative style as that of 'First landing', of how Caesar met and talked to the standard-bearer who led the invasion.

5 Write an account of the ways in which the battle tactics of the Romans and the tribesmen differed.

6 Write a special account of the moment in 'Battle in the sun' when elephants were brought into action. Imagine their effect on the enemy, think of ways in which they could be used most effectively, and describe them in action.

7 Try to imagine what might have happened to Gwydion after he has run through the battlefield. Write your own version to begin at the point where Henry Treece's story stops, with the words: 'and at last something struck him on the head and in the middle of the back, and he knew no more.'

8 Write a page or two of conversation between two Roman legionaries as they wait for the charging tribesmen to reach them. Bear in mind the Romans' attitudes towards their enemies.

Further activities

1 When you have read the description of Britain by Bede, try to imagine how your own local area would have looked at that time: few houses or roads, no neat hedges and fields, and so on. Take a look at a particular scene near your home or school and try to describe it as Bede might have done.

2 Find out as much as you can about your area in Roman times, and about Roman remains there. Local historians, libraries, museums and the Ordnance Survey maps of Roman Britain will all help.

3 Find out what you can about the organization of the Roman legions: what weapons they used, their auxiliary troops and their battle techniques.

Early peace and resistance

9 The brooch

HENRY TREECE

Caradoc was finally defeated in AD 51 and for a few years there was peace. In this passage, Marcus, a young Roman boy, ignores the warnings of his British slave and rides along a road sacred to the native people. He meets Boudicca (or Boadicea, as the Romans called her) the great queen of a British tribe, the Iceni, and tries to live up to the standards of courage expected of him as a Roman.

So he swung his white pony round and dug his heels in the beast's sides and was soon away like the wind. The road was really little more than a mud track, baked hard by the sun, and flanked on either side by tall elders and wild briars, with oak trees above them and, here and there, a flowering thorn. It was exciting to ride this track because suddenly it fell into a steep hollow where the shadows from the trees almost blotted out the sunlight. A hare loped across the road in front of the white pony and for a moment Marcus was almost thrown. But then the track climbed upwards again, before it disappeared round a high bank of ferns.

Marcus put the white pony at this slope gaily, shouting encouragement as he drummed with his heels. Then just as he was at the top and swinging round the ferns, his heart almost jumped into his mouth.

Coming towards him and filling the track were horsemen on shaggy ponies and carrying tall lances. They wore wolf-skins about their shoulders and great iron helmets with bulls' horns at the sides, which made them look very fierce indeed. But it was the woman who rode before them all on a black horse that most startled Marcus, for he had never seen anyone like her in his life. She was dressed like a man, with a wolf-skin jacket and hide-breeches bound round with coloured thongs of braid. Her helmet hung on the saddle-horn and her thick hair flowed on to her shoulders as russet as a fox's pelt. Marcus noticed all the gold rings and bronze bracelets she wore, but what caught his eye most of all was the strange tattoo-mark in the middle of her forehead. It was in the form of a watching eye. And on her cheeks were other streaks of blue, in lines, that gave her a very savage look.

At first he thought she was going to ride him down for she made no effort to pull in her black horse. But just at the last moment, when he was wondering what on earth she would do, she stopped and stared at him silently, her eyes wide open and angry. This made him feel very young and very helpless; but he remembered that his father was a Tribune and so he sat there in the middle of the track and tried to put on the expression of *dignitas.*

And after a very long time the woman leaned a little to one side of her horse's tall neck and said to him in very fair Latin, 'I think you must be ten.'

Marcus smiled, although the woman was not smiling, and said, 'No, I am eight. But I am big for my age.'

The woman said, 'When you speak to me you must say, "My Lady".'

Marcus tried to frown at this, but in the end he said, 'Very well, my lady.'

Then the woman nodded and said, 'That is your first lesson in manners, Roman. Now, since you are eight years old, you should know enough to declare your own name properly.'

This time Marcus felt very stubborn. He said, 'I am not used to telling my name to every stranger I meet on the road, my lady.' He said the last two words very loudly so that she would see the sort of people Romans were. But she did not seem to care and said, 'I am not a stranger, but you are. This is not your road, but it is mine. There are certain words I could say to the warlords who ride with me, and then you would be in a very awkward position indeed. Yes, very awkward. So have the goodness to state your name, aged eight.'

So Marcus gave his name, very crestfallen, and said who his father was, and with whom they were staying. And when he had finished, the woman beckoned him to come closer to her. And when he sat almost beneath her shadow, she said, 'I am the Queen here. Can you understand that?'

Marcus nodded, feeling most ashamed now. The woman said,

'My name is Boudicca, which in your language means the Victorious One.'

She waited a while, and to fill in the silence, Marcus said, 'Then, my lady, I am sorry that I galloped along your road. I thought that it looked exciting. That is all.'

The Queen stared at him for a while with a frown on her forehead. Then she said strangely, 'Yes, it is exciting to many who go down it. It is so exciting that they wish they might never come to the end of it, but that they could fly away like birds straightaway.'

Then for the first time Marcus noticed that, at the end of the column of horsemen, there was a man on foot. His wrists were tied and he had a wound on one side of his head. It was unbandaged and the flies were troubling the man, but the horsemen didn't seem to mind.

Marcus said, 'What had that poor man done, my lady? He looks very sad.'

For a moment Queen Boudicca frowned again, this time quite angrily. But then she shook her head and smiled. 'I do not ask you about your private affairs, do I?' she said. 'I do not ask you who showed you this road, do I?'

Marcus said stoutly, 'If you did I shouldn't tell you.' Then at the last moment he remembered to say, 'My lady.'

Suddenly the Queen seemed to lose all interest in him. She called out to the warlords in a harsh language and they prepared to ride on. Then she looked down at Marcus again and felt in the deerskin pouch at her side. In her hand she held a round bronze brooch, on which was moulded a shape like a stag leaping, but all done in strips of metal joined together so that, unless you looked very carefully, you could not tell what it represented.

She held this brooch out to the boy and said, 'This is for you. It is the queen's brooch and will serve to hold up your cloak when you are bigger. Do not lose it for it might be very useful to you one day. Suppose, for instance, you were galloping along my road another time and the men caught you and wanted to punish you—then you could show them this brooch and they would know that the Queen had given you her permission to go where you wished in Iceni territory. That would be useful, wouldn't it?'

But before Marcus could answer, she said quite sternly, 'Now move out of my way and let me pass, Roman.'

From *The Queen's Brooch*

10   The Roman villa in England

CECIL ROBERTS

With peace, some Romans and wealthy Britons built villas. These were often expensive buildings, especially in the later years of the Roman occupation, but here a poet suggests that not even these solid buildings could withstand the effects of time.

How clever those Roman fingers
　　Working here,
Now only a little lingers
　　From that far year;
When last this pavement sounded,
　　Hadrian spoke,
The trireme galleys grounded,
　　From the hearth rose smoke.

How little has the landscape altered,
　　These uplands green
Where Claudius' cattle faltered;
　　And there between
Those fallen posts, now crumbled,
　　The chariot ran,
The Roman street once rumbled
　　With the traffic of man.

How futile the hopes they nourished,
　　Foolish indeed,
For, even as they flourished,
　　There grew Time's seed

To split their stones asunder,
    However firm,
And, ruinously, deep under,
    Worked the lowly worm.

From *Selected Poems*

11 Dolphin mosaic

IAN SERRAILLIER

The villas themselves have disappeared but their floors often remain with their elaborate mosaic patterns. In this poem, such a floor is found, after hundreds of years, by a lucky accident.

This stone mosaic picture—shells, vases,
Wild creatures bounding through a summer sea.
He sat the boy astride a dolphin's back,
Trident in hand, with wings to steady him;
He made twin horses, to gallop the waves with wings;
Twin panthers too, with tails and prancing paws;
And last, on the leafy border, a lonely bird.

The craftsman sighed when his joyful work was done.
'I'm tired,' he said, 'of this wet and shivering land.
Tomorrow I sail for home.' Then Roman families came;
They walked on the square sea, they lay on couches
To dine and drink; the little grandson of the house
Fell sprawling on the floor and broke his goblet.
After a hundred years, a cry of, 'Fire!
The palace is ablaze from end to end!'
A cloud of smoke, drips of molten lead,
Falling tiles and nails and window glass,
And rafters shooting flame . . . Slowly,
Through centuries of silence, the earth surged in,
Hiding the picture from the ploughman's sight.

Then someone shouted, 'The trench for the water-main—
We'll dig it here!' A noise of engines,
Then the digging stopped. Careful fingers

Scraped the earth away; astonished eyes
Gazed at the dolphin boy, the stony sea,
The horses and the panthers and at last,
There in the leafy border, the lonely bird.

From *Miscellany Six*

12 Shoes for a princess

JOHN JAMES

Not all the wealthy and noble Britons followed Roman fashions. Mediterranean merchants had traded in southern Britain for many years. Here, one of them, a Greek called Plotinus, sells shoes in a local market and meets a native princess in all her finery.

'Now for shoes like these, what would you say was a fair price? What do I say? Twenty-five silver denarii a pair? Would not that be fair? But am I asking twenty-five denarii a pair? I, who only came here to benefit my kinsmen? I who only came here to make you remember, and remember kindly, your brethren in Galatia?

'Shall I ask you twenty denarii a pair, then? Shall I even ask for ten denarii a pair? No!! I have come to invite you to share in my own good fortune, because I walk in such shoes every day of my life. Shall I ask for five denarii a pair, that would hardly cover the cost of the leather and the dye, and leave nothing over to reward us for our labour? No!!! All I need here is enough money in my hand to pay for the night's lodgings for myself and my friend, and for a handful of musty hay for our horses, who are religious and given to fasting. All I ask is two denarii, just two little horses, for a pair of the most durable, the most comfortable, the most distinctive shoes you will ever wear.'

They sold like water in a city under siege. Long before noon we had sold almost all our stock, and I was already beginning to reckon up my profit—I estimated that I had made three pairs for less than one denarius. All kinds of people had come to buy, first the market people themselves, and then farmers and their wives, and our greatest sale had, as always, been among the local lads buying what they hoped would get their girls into the long grass with them. But then as I looked at my last pair, a different customer arrived. There

40

was a sudden thinning out of the crowd in front of me, leaving a space, and as I looked it was covered with a swarm of sparrows, hopping about and quarrelling for the crumbs and the grains of oats they found in the horse-droppings. And as I looked down, there appeared among the birds the feet of a Lady. It was feet and shoes I was looking at that day, and by the shoes this was a great Lady, the litter trade if ever I saw it. They were fine and dainty feet, and that was real Spanish leather that covered them, and dyed it was in a dye that would stand up to all the weather of the world. Dressed she was like a woman of the country. Not like the women of Pontes, who wanted to show how sophisticated they were and walked Roman fashion in tunics with a pallium to throw over their shoulders if the weather required it, which it always does up there.

I saw beneath her skirt of wool, fine wool, all woven in a check of light blue and dark blue and grey, there were a dozen petticoats. Each one was of a different colour. I raised my eyes to her apron, of fine linen, white, and embroidered with the flowers of the flax. This linen I knew, it had come from Egypt. About her waist was her belt, and this if not the belt of a queen was the belt of a queen's daughter or of a queen to be, for it was of a dozen strands of chain, alternate links of Gold and silver, and at the front it was fastened by a buckle of silver, the size of both my palms, studded with garnets. I looked farther up, to the full bosom hidden, half hidden, by a blouse of silk, white silk, but embroidered in its turn with blue silk in a Pictish pattern of whorls and spirals. I looked up to her shawl, and this was of cotton, white again, and tasselled, and it was woven through and across with golden wire, and the wire ran out to stiffen the tassels. And under the shawl I saw hair of a light lively red, and it framed a face well known, well known indeed.

There she stood like a rich and splendid trireme, beating back from a voyage to the Seres, all laden with silk and Gold and pearls and diamonds. Rich enough she was to buy up all the ocean, strong enough to beat off all attack. She stood before me with her flags and banners flying, her birds sang about her like a cloud of sail full drawing. And she spoke, in a voice that I surely had heard singing:

'How much for shoes, Mannan?'

At the sound of that voice, all my bones turned to water. Somewhere deep down inside me the merchant said, 'Go on, tell her the tale, how they are dyed by a secret recipe known only to the ancients of Galatia, and how they would be cheap at a hundred denarii, and how you will reduce them for her, special for her, to a mere twenty-five.' But I could not do it. I looked at that oval face, the straight nose and the firm lips, and I looked down to where it looked back at me from my own shoes, and all I could say was:

'For you, my Lady, there is no charge. They are a gift. Take them as an offering to your beauty from your brethren in Galatia.'

She stood still a moment. Then she called over her shoulder:

'Pay him, Hueil.'

A man came forward from the crowd behind, and I saw that he was wearing trousers in the same blue and grey check as her skirt, and more, that he was one of a group, four or five. He came to me, and picked up the last pair of shoes, then shook his head and threw them back on the ground. Then he stooped to where I squatted cross-legged, and in one swift movement whipped the shoes off my feet, the shoes on which I had painted Aphrodite, and stuffed them into his bag. He tossed me, contemptuously, a coin, and followed his mistress into the crowd.

From *Not for all the Gold in Ireland*

13   A Roman legion

G. M. DURANT

To maintain the uneasy peace in their province of Britannia, the Romans needed a well-trained army. Here, a modern historian describes the organization of a Roman legion and the life of its men.

Ideally there were 6,000 fighting men in a legion, divided into ten cohorts which were each sub-divided into six centuries. Originally, every legionary, who was always an infantryman, had to be a Roman citizen; but this qualification meant little after the Emperor Caracalla at the beginning of the third century (210) granted Roman citizenship to every freeborn person in the Empire. In any case, in imperial times soldiers were not so easily come by that such a limitation could be adhered to; we find that even as early as the second century Britons were becoming legionaries—in the legions stationed in Britain—as well as auxiliaries. Nor had there ever been any limitation on promotion. A legionary of ability, if he wished, could rise from the ranks through a series of grades to become, eventually, a centurion.

The centurions, the commanders of the centuries, were the backbone of the Roman army. That army was famed far and wide, admired by friends and feared by foes, for its strict discipline, its drilled efficiency, its training; and it was the centurions who were responsible for its drill and training, and who enforced discipline. In times of battle they also commanded and led their century of 100 men in the attack. The most able of them might rise further, and become prefects or tribunes, who commanded the auxiliaries.

The cohorts of auxiliaries, commanded by prefects (*praefecti*), were not, at this time, parts of the legion. They were the provincials fighting in their native garb and with their native weapons on the frontiers of Europe. They were considered irregular troops, without the status of the legionaries. They served for a term of twenty-five years (the legionary's was twenty) and their pay was less; and as they were stationed on the frontiers they often bore the brunt of any enemy attack. They were quartered in small forts along the line of the frontier; in Britain we find them for a while on the Antonine Wall, and for over three centuries on the Wall of Hadrian.

These auxiliaries had in earlier days been recruited from among newly conquered tribes, and they kept the name of their tribe, and were referred to as the 'first cohort of Batavians', or the 'second cohort of Thracians', or if they were cavalry units, the 'first *ala* of Asturians', and so on. It was not the normal rule, however, for them to serve in their native territory, possibly owing to the encouragement that might have given for mutiny and armed revolt against the Romans. They were sent to another part of the Empire altogether. So we find, garrisoning the forts along Hadrian's Wall, Asturians from Spain, Tungrians from what is now Belgium, Thracians, Sarmatians, Batavians, Dalmatians and others, while levies raised in Britain might be found as far off as the frontier-line along the Danube. But, as the auxiliaries settled down on some frontier—for instance, in Britain—men to fill gaps in a unit caused by death or retirement tended to be recruited not from the original foreign tribe which had given its name to the cohort, but from the local population. Furthermore the auxiliaries often married local women (until the end of the third century serving soldiers were not allowed to marry, but any liaisons they made were officially recognized as legal marriages on their retirement, and the children of the union were considered legitimate); sons frequently followed the profession of their fathers, and after a time a cohort or *ala* of auxiliaries bearing the name of some foreign tribe would be likely to contain many native-born soldiers. At the end there would probably be more British cavalrymen in the first *ala* of Asturians than Spaniards, and most of the infantrymen in the second cohort of Thracians would be Brigantes.

All these soldiers, legionaries and auxiliaries alike, spoke Latin. They had to, for it was the language of command. But we should be mistaken if we thought of it as Ciceronian Latin. 'Army Latin' would be a better name for it, and the modern languages derived from it, French, Spanish, Italian and Rumanian, occasionally give us glimpses of its deviations from the classical. Let two examples illustrate the point. When the army referred to somebody's head, it does not seem to have used the classical word *caput*, but *testa*, meaning a tile or potsherd, later a skull. This was adopted by the Gauls as the only word for the object, and it ended up as *tête*. Also, a horse was not *equus* to the army, but *caballus*, a rather derogatory word for the animal, becoming through Gaulish, the normal French *cheval*.

A legionary had to be able to march twenty miles in five hours, carrying all his kit, which included, besides three days' rations and his mess-tin, a saw, an axe, an entrenching tool, and a wicker basket for the earth he threw up when digging the prescribed ditch around the night's camp; for even when it stayed only one night in a spot the Roman army always measured out and fortified an entrenched camp. The Roman soldier also had to be a regular commando, able to scale barriers, vault fences, leap across ditches and swim rivers and straits—we remember how Agricola required this of his troops when he crossed to Anglesey—and to take part in the rapid erection of temporary camps and fortifications. They were also trained to be masons capable of building a stone wall; for it was the legions, as we remarked before, not slaves, who raised Hadrian's Wall. But there were also, attached to every legion, specialist engineers, surveyors and sappers; while ordinary soldiers might, if they chose, specialize as signallers, armourers, medical orderlies, clerks and accountants. A legion was a self-contained unit and could do everything for itself.

From *Britain, Rome's Most Northerly Province*

14 Song of the Ninth (Hispana) Legion

HENRY TREECE

A Roman soldier's life was a hard one. This poem gives some idea of the coarse humour of the soldiers, their pride in their own legion and their contempt for the other legions of the army.

The Fourteenth asks for glory,
The Twentieth asks for meat;
The Second asks soft slippers
To ease its tired feet;

But the Ninth wants none of these things;
It does not fight for gain;
It only asks a pair of feet
To march back home to Spain.

It only asks a pair of hands
To dig a bloody road;
And a pair of bloody shoulders
To lift a bloody load;

It only asks a girl a day
To help the hours to pass,
And a well-shod pair of army boots
To kick the Second's arse!

From *Red Queen, White Queen*

15 A noble death

HENRY TREECE

The early peace was broken and the legions marched and fought again. In AD 61 Boadicea rebelled and led the natives through south-east England towards London, sacking Colchester on the way. Here one soldier fights to the end as a true Roman should, and is saluted by his enemies.

Marcus looked to where the centurion pointed and saw something that he would never forget. Above the river, in one of the square gardens of a ruined house, a grey-haired veteran stood on a heap of straw and turfs with a wooden shovel in his hands. He used it like an axe on all who came at him; and each time a dark-faced enemy fell back, this old man laughed gently and called out a number. They heard his voice clearly from where they stood. 'Nine,' he called. 'Now, come on, little ones, and let me make it ten. What, have I marched all the way from Persia to be denied ten? Why, when I was in my prime, lads, under the main Eagle of the Second, I could manage ten before I went back to the tents for my morning porridge!'

Marcus said shortly, 'I am going to him.'

But the centurion dragged him back. 'You fool,' he said. 'You would never cross that river. Be still, he has made up his mind what will happen. He would not even thank you to rob him of this last moment. I have felt this many times, under the Eagles in Batavia and Gaul and Africa. It is nothing; it is what a centurion expects at the end. This man was a centurion. Look at the way he set himself. Boy, only a centurion stands like that.'

Now the dark tribesmen lay back, waiting by the garden wall, some of them grinning up at the old warrior, some of them feeling their arms and legs in pain. The vast crowds about the city, in the trampled fields, sat silent, their eyes wide, their mouths open, many of them weeping without shame.

Then in this strange moment of silence, the voice of Boudicca herself sounded on the heavy air. Marcus could not see where she was, but he heard her words plainly enough. She said, 'Old man, old man, it is a waste of bravery for such as you to die. We of the Iceni would stand ashamed in the eyes of the Mother if we put an end to you. I beg you, come forward and take my hands in homage, and you shall be among the first of my captains.'

But the old man only glanced towards her and laughed. Then, in a thin calm voice he said for all to hear, 'Who is prating about the Mother? Is there no Mithras to call on? He is the man's god, the soldier's friend. Is there some stray cat among you, yowling down there by the river? Let her come up here and have her tail trimmed.'

Now the tribesmen seated about the city began to smile and then to laugh, at first quietly and then openly, so that their laughter swept across the city like a gust of wind.

And Marcus suddenly heard a thin squeal of the Queen's bone whistle, and then in the middle of the old veteran's grey linen tunic a short arrow stood out. He heard the little thud it made, though he was so far away, and thought he heard the old man draw in his breath.

For a while the veteran stood on the heap of turf, tottering, still with his hands clenched about his shovel, still trying to laugh. And then even he had to listen to the dark god's summoning. He swayed and let fall his shovel. Then one of his legs gave way and caused him to totter backwards down the heap. A dark-skinned man started forward, his lance in his hand; but the chieftain beside him struck this man a hard blow that sent him back like a beaten dog.

And those in the garden and those about the city watched this old Roman go on to his knees, and then on to his face, and then spread out his thin arms as though he knew at the last that he could not fight all the world. And all of them saw that he was still laughing when his face plunged suddenly into the straw.

And when this was over, the tribes about the city sighed and beat with their hands upon their hard thighs in admiration. And the sound they sent up stirred the birds from the trees for a mile on every side.

And before these birds had settled again, Marcus suddenly cried out, 'What he can do, we can, brother! Come, let us try these British jackals.' He started to run, and so Tigidius followed him.

From *The Queen's Brooch*

16   The desertion of London

STEPHANIE PLOWMAN

The Roman army was forced to desert even the city of London before the British onslaught. In this extract, a young officer describes the horror of abandoning Roman Londinium and its people to the mercy of Boadicea.

Let me speak in the third person of our abandonment of London. It is easier that way. Why is it so difficult to speak of London when I could write personally of Colchester? Because I fought for Colchester, I took part in her agonies. I left London.

They had been afraid in London, very much afraid, when the weary, blood-stained survivor from Colchester rode down from the north. When he had grimly ordered the men to widen and deepen the ditch, ordered the women to take their children and get out of London, hide in the marshlands to the south, scatter among the forests to the north, but get out of London at all costs, they had obeyed, tearfully, reluctantly, but docilely. They had hidden household treasures, they had taken babies from cradles, wondering how they would sleep through the dark nights in hiding, the women wailing a little themselves in fear and grief. But then the cavalry had appeared in a flurry of flying red cloaks, and a jingle of bronze and steel. The Londoners who had delayed came running out then, to stare eagerly at the big troopers with their flushed, fair, smiling faces, at the Governor erect on his black horse, embodiment of Roman power, the man who had made the crossing to the Druids' legendary stronghold. Surely he would deal easily enough with these Britons of the south-east, who had been conquered by Rome in the past? A sudden spirit of wild optimism ran through the Londoners; next, the name of Cerialis was on every lip, Cerialis who marched and fought with the speed and shock of lightning. Cerialis

49

who must have done the job already. No one knew who started that story, but most people accepted it. Men hurried out of the town to bring back their families. Bundles were unpacked, children stopped crying, babies, lulled by the familiarity of their cradles, slept at last.

Friendly Britons welcomed the returning refugees, helped settle them back in their homes, said comfortably that digging the trench was so much wasted time, that Boudicca would never get to London, that the survivor from Colchester, poor fellow, wasn't right in the head, and, understandably enough, exaggerated the number of rebels, out of all sense. The truth was, Cerialis must have dealt with the situation, was probably in Caistor already. Quite soon after the Governor's arrival, the little groups of watchers had drifted away from the main gates; only one Londoner saw a handful of Batavians returning from patrol to the north, no one saw a dispatch rider coming in wearily from the west. But an hour before midnight, after re-settling their families back in the homes they had not thought to see again, many people came out once more to roam through the streets, laughing, talking excitedly. By a natural impulse most of them congregated outside the headquarters building. They cheered when the Governor came out to speak to them. He found it difficult to get silence.

He told them that the Second would not come, and that the Ninth, which had tried to come, could not. With his tiny force of cavalry, he himself could not defend London; he must retire up Watling Street, to link up with the advancing Fourteenth. Any man fit to bear arms might march with him, but no one else, for all rested on endurance, and he could not take food supplies for useless mouths. The women and children, the old and the sick, must do what they had already been told, get out of London, get to the forests, or over the bridge while it still remained, and find refuge in the flood plain to the south; but they must make haste, for London Bridge was going down as fast as axes could get it down. He himself was moving out as soon as the military stores and supplies had been destroyed.

But the Londoners did not scatter. They stood there looking at him as inert, as voiceless as if they were already dead. They watched apathetically as troopers moved through the doomed streets, burning storehouses, throwing supplies into the river. They saw the bridge go crashing down. They heard a trumpet sounding. Some of the men started at that call, moved off, to follow the little force of cavalry as it drew off to the north-west.

And then as we passed through that pathetic unfinished rampart and ditch, we heard it, the death-cry of London. From the throats of those thousands of doomed creatures that we had left to death and torment came a long continuous moan, a sound I shall never forget, that I often hear even now, in nightmares, a sound of lost souls accusing their betrayers, a despairing wail that still sickens my spirit. I rode at the rear with Civilis, and he rode blindly, tears raining down his face, cursing and praying alternately. At last he said, 'When I was a little boy, there was a ship wrecked just off the shore one night, a big ship, a transport, I think, and from the men struggling in the sea there came a noise—like that—'

After a moment he added, 'But this is worse,' and began cursing and weeping again, and saying that *then* it was a night of storm, but tonight was a calm night and still, with the stars bright and peaceful.

And indeed the stars shone calmly on us as we rode forward, some of us dropping the reins, with our hands up to our ears to shut out that dreadful crying sound, and I, for one, wondering how much pain the frail body of a woman or a child can endure before death brings relief.

From *To Spare the Conquered*

17 Here the legion halted

JOHN MASEFIELD

In this poem by John Masefield a Roman soldier, faced with next day's battle, considers the triviality of a quarrel among his comrades.

Here the legion halted, here the ranks were broken,
And the men fell out to gather wood;
And the green wood smoked, and bitter words were spoken,
And the trumpets called to food.

And the sentry on the rampart saw the distance dying
In the smoke of distance blue and far,
And heard the curlew calling and the owl replying
As the night came cold with one star;

And thought of home beyond, over moorland, over marshes,
Over hills, over the sea, across the plains, across the pass,
By a bright sea trodden by the ships of Tarshis,
The farm, with cicadae in the grass.

And thought, as I: 'Perhaps, I may be done with living
To-morrow, when we fight. I shall see those souls no more.
O beloved souls, be beloved in forgiving
The deeds and the words that make me sore.'

From *Collected Poems*

18 How stilts came to the Fens

W. H. BARRETT

Boudicca was eventually defeated, and the Romans drove the tribes
back. Many escaped to the Cambridge fens to carry on the battle
in rather unusual ways, as we learn in this extract from *Tales from
the Fens*.

Have I got a pair of stilts? Of course I have, and if you want to see
them, look in my shed and you'll find a pair there, made out of the
best bit of ash wood that was to be got when they were made, and
that's a tidy while ago. They were given to my grandfather by his
grandfather, and I've had them for over seventy years, so they've
been knocking about a good while. Yes, I can walk with them,
leastways I think I can, as I haven't been up on them for twenty
years. It took a bit of practising to get the use of them because the
foot rest's five foot from the ground, so a man standing on them has
his eyes about ten foot and a half up in the air. They're a job to get
on to, too, and that's why you can still see some of those old wooden
blocks outside some of the houses; you had to stand on them to get
on to the stilts. And if you fell off, then you had to stay off till you
found a bit of bank to stand on to get on again. It's a funny thing,
but we still talk about stilts even if we don't use them any more.
When you see a man lying on the ground, so drunk he can't get
up, then you say he's stilted. And when a farmer can't make a do of
things and he's up to his eyes in debt, then the people he owes money
to come and knock him off his stilts, when they sell him up. But you
were wanting to know why folk round here first had stilts; well, if
you don't get in too much of a hurry to pull your ell lines in, I'll
tell you.

Hundreds of years ago, as I've told you before, all the fen was
under water; that was in winter. In summer the ground dried up

53

when the water had drained away, so after a few warm days, what had been stinking black mud was soon covered over with a green grass. It was something like twitch, that grass, because its roots ran right through the peat and into the clay, and it grew so fast that, in a few weeks, it was seven or eight feet high. It had a stem that was very tough, and on the stem were long spikes of grass which was wonderful stuff for horses and cattle to feed on. It was so rich because, when the fen was flooded, all the fish dung worked right down into the clay where the roots of the grass were. Now, when those Romans came, this part of the fen was always fed off by the horses that pulled the chariot of the Queen [Boudicca] who used to rule over these parts. But all of it wasn't fed off, some of it was left to run to hay, and the Queen's men used to cut it before the rains came and carry it up to the high ground and stack it there. Then, in winter, they used to cut it out and bale it and send it by boat to wherever the Queen had her stables, up on the high ground.

When the Romans got to Cambridge a lot of them started moving out into the Fens and, like they do today, the soldiers weren't long in finding out where the women were. So many of them started courting, and didn't come back, that the captain in Cambridge saw that, if he didn't get a move on, it wouldn't be long before he'd have to do all by himself any fighting that wanted doing. So he sent word to a pal of his living by the sea on the other side of Lynn to send all the boats he had by him and to make a clean sweep of the Fens. Then he wrote to another pal, out Yarmouth way, telling him to meet him the other side of Thetford and to clear up everything as he went along, and he'd do the same himself, on his way up from Cambridge. Well, do you know, boy, for a whole week the sky was lit up at night by the fires they made, burning everything up as they went along. And after the captain's two pals had met, they worked their way into Essex and were lucky enough to lay hands on the Queen and her four daughters, and they treated them the same as they'd treated the other women; then they went back to their camp. But they'd stirred up such a fuss that it wasn't long before the Queen's men gathered round her and told her they'd follow her to hell and back again, if she'd lead them. She told them she would but, before they set out, they'd better have a drink; so they sat down and great big gotches of mead were handed out.

Well, I don't know how strong that mead was, but it must have had a lot of go in it because, before the week was out, the only

Romans left living were those who were running away, trying to hide up. Some of them got into the Fens, and when Father was claying, down Redmere way, he and his mate dug up six of them, all wearing iron shirts, and six heads were lying by themselves, showing that somebody had done a good bit of work for the Queen. Then, after a rest, the Queen's men went back to her and told her that, with a good fill-up of mead inside them and her in her chariot in front, they reckoned they could clear the whole country of those Romans. She said it was a good idea but a bit risky, but, after taking a good swig from the gotch, she jumped in her chariot and was off, hell for leather. They made a good journey till they ran into a solid wall of Roman soldiers, and when the Queen's men found that it wasn't any good trying to throw themselves against that wall any longer, the Queen told them to turn and make for home.

But, just as she was trying to turn her chariot, to go back with them, one of the traces slipped, so she got out to put it on again. Before she could get back, her horses bolted and she was left standing, and before she could get out of the way the Roman soldiers were atop of her and she was trampled into the ground.

It wasn't long before the whole fen after that was smothered with Roman soldiers who ripped the guts out of every man they could get hold of; and it was the same on the high ground, too. And they rounded up all the women and, to keep them out of mischief, they set them to build a road across the fen, starting at Denver and going right through to Peterborough. It must have been pretty hard work because, when they were dredging the Hundred Foot, some time ago now, they came across some of the foundations of that road, and they were slabs of stone that took four men to lift them. They were all summer on that job of road-building and, as all the soldiers helping the women were horse-soldiers, they all turned out their horses to graze on what we call Horse Fen now; and when they went back to camp the general wanted to know what those horses had been fed on to make them so sleek and fat. When he was told it was the fen grass that made them like that, he said he must go down to the Fens himself next spring, which he did. So, all next summer, thousands of horses came down to graze. A lot of them were like horses are today, finding the sweetest bits are on the edge of boggy ground, so a good many of them slipped in, and the soldiers found they'd lost their horses in the peat.

Next summer, when the soldiers came down into the Fens again with their horses, they were told to stop with them to see they didn't get bogged up; if they did fall in, then the men were to get them out before they sank right into the clay. Those soldiers who were told to do this weren't fighting soldiers; they were the foot soldiers who did all the dirty jobs, like mucking out the stables, getting the straw and hay in and things like that. They weren't so tall as the other men so, when the horses were feeding in the tall grass, they couldn't see them. If they followed the horses into the middle of the fen, then they got lost and had to keep walking round and round, trying to find their way out. This was a bad job for them because the few Fenmen who were left used to creep up behind them. Then, before they knew what was happening to them, those soldiers would be out of the army for good, and the Fenmen had another good spear or sword to carry on the good work with. This happened so often that the chap who was doing the cooking found he had more grub than there were soldiers to eat it, so he thought the best thing was for the captain to come down and count his men, to stop good grub from being wasted.

When the captain had done that, he found a lot of his men were missing so he marched the rest up to the high ground and sent down some horse soldiers in their place, and he gave them orders they were not to get off their horses, except to eat and sleep. Well, these new chaps were really worse off than the others had been because they kept galloping about and not looking where they were going so, before they knew where they were, not only was another horse bogged down but a man as well. And if the man did manage to clamber out, it wasn't long before he was back where his horse was and a Fenman was making his way to the high ground, where there was a chap in a wood who bought army swords and saddles to sell to those who'd lost theirs.

When the horses were taken back to camp again and the soldiers had been counted in, so many were missing that the general in charge was sent back to Rome, where they made a great fuss over the way he'd been handling things, and he was thrown out of the army. So he turned himself into a priest and came back here and built a temple of his own with a statue of Venus in it, and before long he was one of the richest men in the place where Cambridge stands now. I've been told that, when they were getting the foundations out for Girton College, they found bits of a temple and inside they dug up a statue of Venus, but that's only what I've heard.

Navvy Ward, who died last year, told me and he worked on that job. He said every shovelful of soil had to go over a screen, and he reckoned there was over a sackful of money dug up, which a chap from one of the colleges told him had been left by the Roman soldiers. Navvy said it wasn't worth much because he took a handful of it when no one was looking, and when he passed a couple of coins over for a pint, the landlord told him to take his dud stuff somewhere else.

Now, when that general had been thrown out, another one was sent down to the Fens in his place. This one had been brought up in the marshes just outside Rome and when he saw the Fens he said they reminded him of home. He brought a fresh lot of men along with him and he told them they'd have to have eyes at the back of their heads, because the place was full of hairy devils who crept up behind any Roman soldier they came across, and knocked him into the bog. But the new lot weren't worried about that, because they'd all done a special training with a pair of long poles, with a step to stand on half-way up and when they were on these they could walk five feet up in the air, and every step they took was the same length. And they'd done so much drilling that they could keep up on these poles for hours, and could even sit back and rest, because they carried another long pole, and when they stuck one end of it in the ground they could sit on the other end, just like they did in the marshes at home.

Well, when spring came and the horses came galloping back into the fen just as it was getting dark, the Fenmen went to bed and dreamed of all the horsekeepers' throats they were going to slit. But when they looked out at daylight they all went and hid up, thinking that what they saw could only mean that the giants, who used to live in the Fens, had come back again. Presently they plucked up their courage, though, and crept up to the high ground, but they were scared out of their wits when they saw dozens of men's heads and shoulders sticking out of the tall grass and reeds, some of them walking about and some standing still. This was something the Fenmen had never seen before, so they all went into the wood and found the sword and spear shop open, because the man who kept it had heard the horses coming back and had got up early in case anything was brought along to the shop. When the men told him what they'd seen he said he was closing down and flitting before the giants got him. Then they suddenly heard a noise, so they all hid

E

up, but it was only one of the Fenmen who'd brought along three long poles as well as a sword and an iron shirt. He said he'd picked them up from the side of a soldier who was having a sleep on some reeds, and he'd left him still fast asleep, with his throat slit from ear to ear. He'd only just managed to cover the body up with reeds when two more poles came along, and there'd been a man standing half-way up them so that only his head and shoulders showed above the grass, and if it hadn't been for the iron shirt he had on, he'd have sworn it was the devil himself, on crutches. And he told them he'd seen a lot of other soldiers, all half-way up in the air, and in one place four of them got off the poles to get a horse out, which had fallen into a dyke, and when it was out they tried to get back on the poles, but they couldn't. So he'd followed them and seen them climb on to a stack of reeds and then get on the poles again and go off, taking such long steps that he'd had to run to keep up with them.

After they'd heard all this, the Fenmen sat down in the wood and had their dinner, and while they were having it they wondered what they could do to catch those soldiers who were walking about like cranes. After the grub was gone and the gotch was empty, a chap called Thoughtful (he'd been given that name because he was always thinking things out), got up and picked up the sword and cut one of the poles into two bits. He told the others that they were unloading sticks and, if they went into the fen with him, he'd show them how to use them. It wasn't long before he and his mates were sneaking through the reeds, where they hid up and waited for a soldier to come along; and in a moment or so one did. He passed just by where the Fenmen were hidden, then he stopped and put his carrying stick behind him and leaned back to have a good look at the fen. But it was his last look, because Thoughtful crept up behind with his unloading stick, knocked away the pole that the soldier was leaning on, and toppled him over backwards, and before he was half-way down, Thoughtful jabbed his sword in him to help him on to the ground. Then he took off the man's shirt, picked up his sword and the poles and went back to his mates to tell them how the idea had worked out. Next morning all the Fenmen went out with unloading sticks and hid in the reeds, with a sword laying handy near by, and by evening, when the bugle blew to tell the soldiers it was supper-time, so many didn't turn up that the chap blew again, thinking they hadn't heard it the first time.

Well, so many soldiers came to pick up those who'd been knocked off their poles that the Fenmen had to lie low for a few days, because a few who did go out were found dangling from three poles tied together at the top with the end of the tie round their necks. When Thoughtful saw them he said that was an idea he'd wanted to get hold of for some time; now he knew how to sling his pot over the fire. And before long the fen was dotted with tripods, only these had soldiers hanging on them to keep them steady. . . .

A few days after this, back in the Fens, a soldier found his way into the wood and went to the shop, hoping to be able to buy a sword as he'd lost his. He saw one just like his old one, so he bought it, and was just turning away when the chap in the shop, who was a Saxon, asked him if he wanted any poles. The soldier said he didn't think so, but he wouldn't mind looking at one or two. When he saw them he said:

'They're not poles, they're stilts.'

'So that's what you call them,' said the Saxon. 'I wondered what they were.'

From *Tales from the Fens*

19 A call to arms

P. CORNELIUS TACITUS

The Romans advanced slowly through what is now England and Wales, and in AD 83 their general, Agricola, attacked Caledonia (Scotland) which was believed to be the northernmost end of the world.

Here, the Roman historian Tacitus reports the speech of the heroic Caledonian chief whom he calls Calcagus, as he rallies the northern tribes for the great battle at Mons Graupius near Inverness, in AD 84.

Whenever I consider why we are fighting and how we have reached this crisis, I have a strong sense that this day of your splendid rally may mean the dawn of liberty for the whole of Britain. You have mustered to a man, and to a man you are free. There are no lands behind us, and even the sea is menaced by the Roman fleet. The clash of battle—the hero's glory—has become the safest refuge for the coward. Battles against Rome have been lost and won before— but never without hope; we were always there in reserve. We, the choice flower of Britain, were treasured in her most secret places. Out of sight of subject shores, we kept even our eyes free from the defilement of tyranny. We, the last men on earth, the last of the free, have been shielded till to-day by the very remoteness and the seclusion for which we are famed. We have enjoyed the impressiveness of the unknown. But to-day the boundary of Britain is exposed; beyond us lies no nation, nothing but waves and rocks and the Romans, more deadly still than they, for you find in them an arrogance which no reasonable submission can elude. Brigands of the world, they have exhausted the land by their indiscriminate plunder, and now they ransack the sea. The wealth of an enemy excites their cupidity, his poverty their lust of power. East and West have

60

failed to glut their maw. They are unique in being as violently tempted to attack the poor as the wealthy. Robbery, butchery, rapine, the liars call Empire; they create a desolation and call it peace.

We instinctively love our children and our kinsmen above all else. These are torn from us by conscription to slave in other lands. . . . Our goods and fortunes are ground down to pay tribute, our land and its harvest to supply corn, our bodies and hands to build roads through woods and swamps—all under blows and insults. Slaves, born into slavery, once sold, get their keep from their masters. But as for Britain, never a day passes but she pays and feeds her enslavers. In a private household it is the latest arrival who is always the butt of his fellow-slaves; so, in this establishment, where all the world have long been slaves, it is we, the cheap new acquisitions, who are picked out for extirpation. You see, we have no fertile lands, no mines, no harbours, which we might be spared to work. Courage and martial spirit we have, but the master does not relish them in the subject. Even our remoteness and seclusion, while they protect, expose us to suspicion. Abandon, then, all hope of mercy and at last take courage, whether it is life or honour that you hold most dear. The Brigantes, with only a woman to lead them, burned the colony, stormed the camp and, if success had not made them grossly careless, might have cast off the yoke. Let us, then, uncorrupted, unconquered as we are, ready to fight for freedom but never to repent failure, prove at the first clash of arms what heroes Caledonia has been holding in reserve.

Can you really imagine that the Romans' bravery in war comes up to their wantonness in peace? No! It is our quarrels and disunion that have given them fame. The reputation of the Roman army is built up on the faults of its enemies. Look at it, a motley agglomeration of nations, that will be shattered by defeat as surely as it is now held together by success! Or can you seriously think that those Gauls or Germans—and, to our bitter shame, many Britons too!—are bound to Rome by genuine loyalty or love? They may be lending their life-blood to foreign tyrants, but they were enemies of Rome much longer than they have been her slaves. Apprehension and terror are weak bonds of affection; once break them, and, where fear ends, hatred will begin. All that can goad men to victory is on our side. The enemy have no wives to fire their courage, no parents ready to taunt them if they run away. Most of them have no country, or, if they have one, it is not Rome. See them, a scanty band, scared and bewildered, staring blankly at the unfamiliar sky, sea and forests around! The gods have given them, spellbound prisoners, into our hands. Never fear the outward show that means nothing, the glitter of gold and silver that can neither avert nor inflict a wound. In the ranks of our very enemies we shall find hands to help us. The Britons will recognize our cause as their own, the Gauls will remember their lost liberty, the rest of the Germans will desert them as surely as the Usipi have just done. They have nothing in reserve that need alarm us—only forts without garrisons, colonies of grey-beards, towns sick and distracted between rebel subjects and tyrant masters. Here before us is their general, here his army; behind are the tribute, the mines and all the other whips to scourge slaves. Whether you are to endure these for ever or take summary vengeance, this field must decide. On, then, into action and, as you go, think of those that went before you and of those that shall come after.

From *Agricola* transl. H. Mattingly

Following on

1 Write an episode in which Marcus, either as a young boy or as a grown man, needs the queen's brooch to save his life.

2 Imagine that you are one of Boudicca's men, riding with her when she meets Marcus. Give your own account of the action in which they had taken the wounded prisoner.

3 Try to imagine what life would have been like for you if you had been the child of a powerful British chief during this time of uneasy peace. If you had been his daughter, perhaps you would have copied Roman women's fashions; if his son, tried to hunt and fight in the Roman style. Imagine that you are such a child, and write an account of a typical day in your life.

4 Other Britons would carry on their resistance to the Romans. Imagine a meeting between a warlike chief who wishes to get rid of the Romans, and one who wants to live in peace. Write what they say to each other, how each behaves, and what each thinks about the future of Britain.

5 Describe the sacking of Colchester by Boudicca's forces as it might have been seen by a Roman who had settled into an easy, peaceful life there.

6 In the same way, imagine and describe various scenes in London shortly after the Roman legions have left.

7 Write an account, in your own local dialect, of your activities as a resistance fighter against the Romans. Imagine how you would use local conditions to defeat them, just as the Fenmen did in 'How stilts came to the Fens'.

The long peace

20 The Roman Wall

ANDREW YOUNG

Though the Caledonian chieftain, Calcagus, was defeated, the Picts
and Scots continued to harry the northern provinces until, in AD
122, the Emperor Hadrian began his famous wall from the Tyne
to the Solway Firth. It remains a massive reminder of the power
of Rome.

Though moss and lichen crawl
    These square-set stones still keep their serried ranks
Guarding the ancient wall,
    That whitlow-grass with lively silver pranks.

Time they could not keep back
    More than the wind that from the snow-streaked north
Taking the air for track
    Flows lightly over to the south shires forth.

Each stone might be a cist
    Where memory sleeps in dust and nothing tells
More than the silent mist
    That smokes among the heather-blackened fells.

Twitching its ears as pink
    As blushing scallops loved by Romans once
A lamb leaps to its drink
    And, as the quavering cry breaks on the stones,

Time like a leaf down-drops
    And pacing by the stars and thorn-trees' sough
A Roman sentry stops
    And hears the water lapping on Crag Lough.

From *Collected Poems 1960*

21 On the Great Wall

RUDYARD KIPLING

The Wall was not the scene of constant fighting between Roman defenders and the northern attackers, but it had to be constantly garrisoned, never a popular prospect for the professional Roman soldier. In this passage from *Puck of Pook's Hill* by Rudyard Kipling, such a man expresses his dismay at what he finds when he arrives at the Wall.

'Of course, the farther North you go the emptier are the roads. At last you fetch clear of the forests and climb bare hills, where wolves howl in the ruins of our cities that have been. No more pretty girls; no more jolly magistrates who knew your Father when he was young, and invite you to stay with them; no news at the temples and way-stations except bad news of wild beasts. There's where you meet hunters, and trappers for the Circuses, prodding along chained bears and muzzled wolves. Your pony shies at them, and your men laugh.

The houses change from gardened villas to shut forts with watch-towers of grey stone, and great stone-walled sheepfolds, guarded by armed Britons of the North Shore. In the naked hills beyond the naked houses, where the shadows of the clouds play like cavalry charging, you see puffs of black smoke from the mines. The hard road goes on and on—and the wind sings through your helmet-plume—past altars to Legions and Generals forgotten, and broken statues of Gods and Heroes, and thousands of graves where the mountain foxes and hares peep at you. Red-hot in summer, freezing in winter, is that big, purple heather country of broken stone.

Just when you think you are at the world's end, you see a smoke from East to West as far as the eye can turn, and then, under it, also as far as the eye can stretch, houses and temples, shops and theatres, barracks and granaries, trickling along like dice behind . . . always behind . . . one long, low, rising and falling, and hiding and showing line of towers. And that is the Wall!'

'Ah!' said the children, taking breath.

'You may well,' said Parnesius. 'Old men who have followed the Eagles since boyhood say nothing in the Empire is more wonderful than first sight of the Wall.'

'Is it just *a* Wall? Like the one round the kitchen-garden?' said Dan.

'No, no! It is *the* Wall. Along the top are towers with guard-houses, small towers, between. Even on the narrowest part of it three men with shields can walk abreast, from guard-house to guard-house. A little curtain-wall, no higher than a man's neck, runs along the top of the thick wall, so that from a distance you see the helmets of the sentries sliding back and forth like beads. Thirty feet high is the Wall, and on the Picts' side, the North, is a ditch, strewn with blades of old swords and spear-heads set in wood, and tyres of wheels joined by chains. The Little People come there to steal iron for their arrow-heads.

But the Wall itself is not more wonderful than the town behind it. Long ago there were great ramparts and ditches on the South side, and no one was allowed to build there. Now the ramparts are partly pulled down and built over, from end to end of the Wall; making a thin town eighty miles long. Think of it! One roaring, rioting, cock-fighting, wolf-baiting, horse-racing town, from Ituna on the West to Segedunum on the cold eastern beach! On one side heather, woods and ruins where Picts hide, and on the other, a vast town—long like a snake, and wicked like a snake. Yes, a snake basking beside a warm wall!!

My Cohort, I was told, lay at Hunno, where the Great North Road runs through the Wall into the Province of Valentia.' Parnesius laughed scornfully. 'The Province of Valentia! We followed the road, therefore, into Hunno town, and stood astonished. The place was a fair—a fair of peoples from every corner of the Empire. Some were racing horses: some sat in wine-shops: some watched dogs baiting bears, and many gathered in a ditch to see cocks fight. A boy not much older than myself, but I could see he was an officer, reined up before me and asked what I wanted.

"My station," I said, and showed him my shield. Parnesius held up his broad shield with its three X's like letters on a beer-cask.

"Lucky omen!" said he. "Your Cohort's the next tower to us,

but they're all at the cock-fight. This is a happy place. Come and wet the Eagles." He meant to offer me a drink.

"When I've handed over my men," I said. I felt angry and ashamed.

"Oh, you'll soon outgrow that sort of nonsense," he answered. "But don't let me interfere with your hopes. Go on to the statue of Roma Dea. You can't miss it. The main road into Valentia!" and he laughed and rode off. I could see the statue not a quarter of a mile away, and there I went. At some time or other the Great North Road ran under it into Valentia; but the far end had been blocked up because of the Picts, and on the plaster a man had scratched, "Finish!" It was like marching into a cave. We grounded spears together, my little thirty, and it echoed in the barrel of the arch, but none came. There was a door at one side painted with our number. We prowled in, and I found a cook asleep, and ordered him to give us food. Then I climbed to the top of the Wall, and looked out over the Pict country, and I—thought,' said Parnesius. 'The bricked-up arch with "Finish!" on the plaster was what shook me, for I was not much more than a boy.'

'What a shame,' said Una. 'But did you feel happy after you'd had a good ——' Dan stopped her with a nudge.

'Happy?' said Parnesius. 'When the men of the Cohort I was to command came back unhelmeted from the cock-fight, their birds under their arms, and asked me who I was? No, I was not happy; but I made my new Cohort unhappy too . . . I wrote my Mother I was happy, but, oh, my friends'—he stretched arms over bare knees— 'I would not wish my worst enemy to suffer as I suffered through my first months on the Wall. Remember this: among the officers was scarcely one, except myself (and I thought I had lost the favour of Maximus, my General), scarcely one who had not done something of wrong or folly. Either he had killed a man, or taken money, or insulted the magistrates, or blasphemed the Gods, and so had been sent to the Wall as a hiding-place from shame or fear. And the men were as the officers. Remember, also, that the Wall was manned by every breed and race in the Empire. No two towers spoke the same tongue, or worshipped the same Gods. In one thing only were we all equal. No matter what arms we had used before we came to the Wall, *on* the Wall we were all archers, like the Scythians. The Pict cannot run away from the arrow, or crawl under it. He is a bowman himself, *he* knows!'

From *Puck of Pook's Hill*

22 Roman Wall blues

W. H. AUDEN

This rather sad little poem by W. H. Auden suggests some reasons
for the ordinary Roman soldier's not liking service at the Wall!

Over the heather the wet wind blows,
I've lice in my tunic and a cold in my nose.

The rain comes pattering out of the sky,
I'm a Wall soldier, I don't know why.

The mist creeps over the hard grey stone,
My girl's in Tungria; I sleep alone.

Aulus goes hanging around her place,
I don't like his manners, I don't like his face.

Piso's a Christian, he worships a fish;
There'd be no kissing if he had his wish.

She gave me a ring but I diced it away;
I want my girl and I want my pay.

When I'm a veteran with only one eye
I shall do nothing but look at the sky.

From *Collected Shorter Poems 1927–1957*

23   The problems of peace

ALFRED DUGGAN

Whatever the state of affairs on the Wall, the Roman occupation of Britain as a whole was not always a matter of fighting. Rules had to be made and forms had to be filled in, as they do in any civilized society. This description of a day in the life of a senior Roman administrator in Londinium shows some of the problems he had to deal with.

The climate of Britain is notoriously vile. But there are occasional fine days, and sometimes they come when they are wanted; otherwise it would be impossible to cultivate the soil of the island, instead of merely very difficult indeed. In the eleventh year of the Emperor Honorius, A.D. 405, the 10th of September was fine; C. Sempronius Felix, Praeses of Britannia Prima, realized that as soon as he woke, from the pattern made by the low sun on the ceiling of his bedroom. At once he thought of the harvest; a wet August had damaged the crops as they were reaped, but a few days of sunshine would dry the ground and enable the farmers to move their wagons between field and barn; they might save more corn than he had been counting on yesterday. He decided to go early to the office, and revise the provisional figures his clerks had made out during the storms of the last month. He threw off the bedclothes and clapped his hands for his valet.

In half an hour he was ready to set out. He was an African from the Mediterranean Sea, where men rise early to work before the heat of midday, and it pleased him to set an example; the provincials were too fond of lying in bed until this beastly island of theirs had warmed up after the chills of the night. He did not waste time on his toilet; it is the privilege of the head of any organization to dress as he pleases when his subordinates have to appear neatly turned out, and there was no one in Londinium who was his superior in rank. Besides, it was the custom of the ancients to bathe after the work of the day, and senior officials should follow ancient custom. He ate a bit of bread and smoked bacon while the valet fastened his tunic, and muttered a very short prayer to the Christian God while his hair was combed over the bald patch. On his way to the stairs he passed the stout door of the women's apartments, now standing open as the housemaids began their work; the eunuch whispered that the Lady Maria was not yet awake, and he did not enter. His young wife usually woke in a bad temper, and it was well to keep out of her way in the early morning; so the early-rising servants did their work very quietly. That was a good thing, though Felix did not really approve of a young lady who was always flogging her maids. However, he had not married Maria for her character, but for her family connections, and he seldom saw her except at meals.

Two footmen waited for him outside. They were hefty, fierce-looking Germans, dressed in what the Divine Gratianus had considered the sort of armour German chiefs would have worn if they had ruled a population of skilled bronze-founders. In fact, they were extremely meek, terrified of infringing a law they did not understand; real soldiers bullied them dreadfully. In the good old days the ruler of a Province was guarded by soldiers, but the Divine Diocletianus had totally severed the civil service from the army; now a Praeses, or even a Vicarius, might not give orders to the most junior recruit. Sometimes Felix regretted that he had lost the power of the sword which Legates had once possessed. But gentlemen were not allowed to join the army, and it was as well that everyone should realize that he had no connection with the hard-drinking profligate boors who held military command in this degenerate age. He strolled along the sunny side of the street with his two attendants following, and tried to see himself as some magistrate of the Republic, a Praetor or a Quaestor, walking through the Sacred City with lictors in his train. It was his favourite daydream, for his education had taught him that the past was a great deal better than the present.

All the same, Londinium was looking very splendid on this fine September morning; architecture was one of the few arts that had improved since the days of the Republic, and this city, unlike most of those in Britain, had not been sacked in the Pictish War. It was very large, a mile long by half a mile wide, and since it had always been the financial capital of Britain (though not the military headquarters) it possessed a fine collection of government offices.

There were few citizens about at this early hour, and those he passed paid little attention to him; the lower classes backed against the wall and cringed in silence, and the more prosperous raised an arm in greeting; but nobody tried to hand him a petition. When he first came to this Province, ten years ago, everyone he met would thrust a paper into his hand, usually wrapped round a bribe; but now they had learned that he never did business outside the office, and that he only took presents after a transaction had been completed, as became an honest official.

It was at this morning hour, before the details of office work had altered the focus of his mind, that he liked to picture the whole Diocese, busy in the cause of Civilization. Here in the peaceful south the coloni grew corn and flax, on the northern moors sheep were sheared, from the western mines came lead and tin; stone must be quarried, fish caught, timber cut and charcoal burned, to supply the wants of the primary producers; there must be enough of every commodity, yet waste must be avoided. All this was the elementary work of the civil service. There should also be a surplus, after paying for defence, to support the sculptors, scholars and poets who were the embodiment of the Good Life of the Oecumene, the interlocking household of the Civilized World. It was much more difficult to find this surplus, and to keep it out of the military pay chest.

The Treasury building was in the old style of the Claudian Emperors, and the columns had been clumsily fashioned by barbarous provincials when the whole place was rebuilt after being burned by the Iceni; that was more than three hundred years ago, and Londinium had not since been sacked by an enemy, though occasionally Roman troops had plundered it in civil war. It was quite an historical monument, though Felix sometimes wished the Picts could have destroyed it in the troubles of forty years ago; then he could have rebuilt in the latest style, with modern conveniences. Nowadays there was more paper work, and the files had to be kept longer; while as most trials were held in private there was no need for the great judgment hall.

The Praeses strode through the portico into his private room off the entrance lobby. Waiting beside his desk, holding a bundle of rolled papers, was Paulinus the freedman, his confidential secretary. Instead of explaining the day's business he plunged into a discussion of the news: 'Good morning, sir. Have you heard anything about the campaign in Italy? or the Irish fleet in the Channel?'

'Nothing fresh, Paulinus. As I told you before, that is good news. If anything had gone wrong the rumour would reach us speedily; but when the army destroys a pack of barbarians that is an everyday occurrence which no one bothers to pass on. We must not gossip about soldiers. What have you got for me there?'

'Rough estimates, sir, of the harvest. The taxgatherers valued it as it was reaped, before it was carried; so we must allow for loss during the late storms. One thing may upset our calculations. If these Irish land and ravage the open country we shall draw no revenue from the south coast this year.'

'Don't bother about that. The Comes Littoris Saxonici is paid an enormous salary to see pirates don't ravage there.'

Felix unrolled the papers, and studied particularly the summary of estimated revenue.

'I see you expect a small surplus, after paying the army,' he said briskly. 'In that case we can do something for education. The law says we ought to have teachers of grammar and rhetoric in large cities, and for the last ten years I have hoped to get them started. I don't like the way the Celtic language is spreading in the country-side; administration is more difficult if the coloni don't understand the instructions of the government. I know there are thousands of other things to be done, but it's hardly worth starting to repair a few roads, when at any moment we may have to stop for lack of funds.'

'Excuse me, sir,' Paulinus said gently. 'If there really is a surplus could we reduce the taxes, or at least forgive some arrears?'

'I certainly can't reduce taxes by my own authority, and the Vicarius would not allow it. For one thing, it would mean endless paper work, probably an application to Mediolanum, before I received permission. I might be rather more gentle with collecting arrears, but they must remain on the file. Have you any particular case in mind? Naturally, taxpayers who are well disposed to the government should be better treated than those who make trouble.'

Felix was a citizen of good birth, descended from a long line of civil servants; it was beneath his dignity to take a bribe. But he knew that freedmen must be judged by different standards. The machine would not work unless the subordinates were willing.

However, his clerk chose to be incorruptible to-day. 'Oh no, sir. I had no particular case in mind, although I know you will always

75

protect my personal friends from the taxgatherers. But the coloni are beginning to desert their land, especially near the coast where they are bothered by pirates. This Province is remarkably free from outlaws at present, but if we press them too hard we shall find Bagaudae starting up, as they have in Gaul.'

'Then the army will deal with them. I am not responsible for order. But I can't reduce the taxes, and you know that as well as I do.'

Paulinus was always trying to earn popularity by taking the side of the taxpayer. It was natural enough, for a successful freedman is loathed by every citizen; had he been harsh as well as successful he would have been lynched long ago. But taxation kept the Empire going; the more taxes were collected, the stronger was the government; and in these days it needed all its strength.

These broad decisions taken, as they had to be taken afresh every day against a perpetual nagging opposition, the Praeses settled down to give judgment on the most urgent of the smaller cases that his subordinates had sent up to him. What should be done with the daughter of a baker who had married a soldier twenty years ago, after the administration had lost track of her during a barbarian raid, and whose three sons now claimed to follow their father into the army? She had clearly broken the law, which made the un-attractive calling of bakery strictly hereditary. She claimed the soldier had taken her by force. That was probably a lie, but it might be true, and it was so long ago there were no witnesses. One solution would be to make her husband put her away, and marry her to a baker on the waiting list for a wife; but the Church would make a fuss about the broken marriage vows. The law said she should be burned alive, now that her crime was at last discovered; but that would do no good to anybody. Of course the military authorities were delighted to find themselves with three prospective native-born recruits, so much cheaper than hired barbarians, and they backed the husband. Perhaps it would be wise to give in gracefully, and put the soldiers under an obligation. In that case the office must check the list of bakers at once, before others decided it was possible to escape their work.

As he had pointed out, Felix was not responsible for order in his Province. But he was responsible for practically everything else. Although Britannia Prima, in the south-east of the island, contained no mines of any metal more precious than iron, Londinium was the port whence most exports were shipped to the Continent; lead, tin, and copper from the west came into the city by wagon or pack-pony, each ingot already stamped with the Emperor's name as a guarantee of weight and purity; small parcels were held in the Treasury until they made up a shipload, and then the chartered merchant ship was sent down river to the fortified port of Rutupiae, to await the right moment for a dash across the pirate-infested Channel. Every mine in Britain belonged to the Emperor, and most of the ore was used in the Imperial workshops and armouries; but for purposes of book-keeping it was convenient to fix its value as it left the Diocese, and this was done in the Treasury of Londinium. In fact, the price of a great many things was fixed in the Provincial Treasury, although for certain classes of goods this was done by the Fiscus at Mediolanum, so that the cost should be the same all over the Oecumene, Sometimes the authorities made a mistake, and the price was found to be uneconomic; this might have led to shortages of goods that were too cheap, but the administration had found a simple remedy. Every occupation necessary to a civilized life was hereditary, from farming to burying the dead; and no one was allowed to change his calling. An increasing proportion of the land was directly farmed by the State, either as the patrimony of some past Emperor or confiscated from an unsuccessful pretender, and the private landowners who remained were so heavily taxed in kind that they were practically in the position of sharecroppers. The government took an enormous proportion of each year's income, and in theory saw it was spent in such a manner that the Province remained civilized and solvent. It was a great responsibility for the civil service, and they worked very hard.

But in practice things did not always go according to plan. In the first place, it was impossible to foresee military expenditure, now that all the barbarians in the world were on the march; if a Praeses saved a little money for next year the soldiers just came and took it, since you cannot make a scheme of defence so perfect that it would not be improved by more expenditure. In the second place, production decreased every year. Citizens were reluctant to marry and breed legitimate children, destined to step into their fathers' shoes; it was simpler to live with a slave girl, and produce offspring who could be sold to pay the taxgatherer. Civilization is only kept in being by unremitting effort, and in the whole Diocese of Britain the citizens seemed to have lost the will to work.

After two hours with his secretary Felix had initialled every urgent paper, and he strolled into the main office to see how his subordinates were getting on. It was a nuisance that Paulinus, the most efficient member of his staff, was a freedman who could not take responsibility; technically he was not a civil servant at all, merely the personal clerk of the Praeses. All officials who had been regularly appointed and were empowered to sign documents were freeborn citizens, and that meant a good deal of work was done twice over. But to-day there was only routine business, which the most junior clerk could deal with; when Felix had done a round of the twenty or thirty desks that administered every activity of the Province of Britannia Prima his work was finished, and it was still only two hours after noon. He could spend the rest of the day bathing and dining, in accordance with the custom of the ancients.

At home he had a quick bath, for he had eaten nothing since his light breakfast at dawn, and though he was accustomed to working on an empty stomach he was always hungry by mid-afternoon. Then he sent to tell his wife he was ready for dinner; the evening could be devoted to social affairs.

From *The Little Emperors*

24 More problems

STEPHANIE PLOWMAN

If civilian life was complicated by administration and form-filling, what of the mighty Roman army?

'. . . the chief discovery of the Roman Army over the past hundred years has been paper-work. The sword rusts in the scabbard—poetic touch—but the tireless pen moves on and on. From the Euphrates to the North Sea orderly rooms are snowed under with forms needing completion in triplicate, the War Office requires a daily return of what each legionary has been occupied in doing —!'
    'Not really, sir!'
    'The sober truth—down it must go, orderly, batman, armoury duty, bath-house fatigue. . . . Then we have to see the poor chaps don't squander their pay, so there are compulsory stoppages for boots, bedding, food, the annual camp dinner, the burial club. From time to time you have to cast your eye over the accounts of the legionary savings-bank, because that's always the department of the standard-bearer, and the virtues that fit him for carrying the eagle don't necessarily involve financial genius. Savings, of course, are compulsory, too; it's one way of stopping desertions. (You think twice about cutting and running for it if it means leaving a large slice of several years' pay in the legionary strong-room.) Then in your spare time you go out tax-collecting on behalf of the civil administration. That's the Army life for you; my own belief is that Achilles took time off from the siege of Troy and stuck to his tent because he'd got behind with his monthly returns of boots, Army, Myrmidons for the use of. . . .'

From *To Spare the Conquered*

25   The soldier's god

D. R. BARKER

In peace and war, soldiers honoured the Roman Eagle and worshipped their gods. This passage from *The Story of Roman Britain*
by D. R. Barker shows why so many soldiers chose Mithras as their
god.

The centurion stepped out of the harsh light and dust of the street
into the cool shade of the temple porch. Great double doors swung
inwards, and he walked through a small, dark room and round a
carved wooden screen, and descended several stone steps into the
nave of the temple. The pungent smell of burning pine cones met
his nostrils, and he could see the acrid smoke swirling up the narrow
shafts of light to little windows set high in the gables. The lamp
behind the sun-ray crown of a statue glowed dimly, throwing
flickering shadows across the width of the nave and on to the benches
on either side. On them he could make out the shapes of old familiar
figures—the Raven, the Persian, the Soldier and several others.
As the Raven showed him to his place on the bench, the centurion
stared thoughtfully and with awe at the great marble altar-piece at
the far end of the nave. On it had been carved the figure of a
god, a magnificent young god, wearing a pointed cap and a flowing
scarlet cloak. He half knelt, half sat on a great bull which struggled
vainly to rise, as the god with one hand pulled back the animal's
muzzle and with the other thrust a knife deep into its neck. The
victor's face though stern was averted, as if he pitied the animal
he was killing, but the marble torch-bearers on either side stood
unmoved by the tragedy, one with his torch up, the other with his
down. They represented life and death, and the god they accompanied was the great god MITHRAS.

Long ago, the centurion believed, Mithras had been created by the god of light, and after a miraculous birth to which had come wondering shepherds, he had slain a great bull from which had sprung all the useful living things of this world. Then, after protecting the world against the powers of darkness, Mithras, his disciples and his faithful ally, the Sun, had partaken of a last supper, and had been finally received into heaven.

Mithras was a noble god and Mithraism was very different from the state religion with its cold, formal bargaining between worshippers and gods who were indifferent to either wickedness or virtue; gods, moreover, who made no attempt to answer the question that had always troubled all men—what happened after death? People like the centurion knew the answer to that question, for had not Mithras shown by his own life that goodness prevailed, and to the just and upright came salvation and immortality?

A good soldier like the centurion was attracted by Mithras' demand that his worshippers should lead honourable and courageous lives; merchants and traders were attracted by the emphasis he laid on honesty and the sanctity of the plighted word, qualities on which their very livelihood depended. But even honourable and upright men could not feel assured of immortality until they had passed various grades of initiation designed to provide proof of their steadfastness and valour.

In all there were seven steps in this ritual, each marked by a name: Raven, Bridegroom, Soldier, Lion, Persian, Courier of the Sun and Father—hence the costumed figures on the bench and each grade was attained only after terrifying ordeals, during which the worshipper might be submitted to prolonged entombment, or led to think he was going to be burnt alive or drowned. At one stage, too, Mithraism seems to have taken over practices followed originally by worshippers of Cybele, the Syrian nature goddess. The worshipper knelt in a shallow pit partially covered with planks. A bull was led on to the planks and killed, and its blood flowed down over the worshipper and cleansed him of all sins, thus ensuring him a second birth.

Wherever the Roman army went Mithraism followed. Mithraic temples were thick along the Rhine where the legions faced the German tribes, and they have also been found in North Africa, Egypt, Syria, Asia Minor and the Balkans. In Britain the garrison of Hadrian's Wall built at least three of these little temples, and near London's Walbrook wealthy merchants and legionaries worshipped together in the fine temple which was excavated recently. But among the ordinary population converts to Mithraism were probably few. For many the Mithraic ritual was far too complicated, and the demands made by Mithras far too great—they preferred to seek an easier road to heaven. There were, too, no fiery Mithraic missionaries to strive to bring the unconverted into the fold. Mithras was worshipped by tight, smug, little groups convinced that they alone were saved, and quite willing to let the rest of the world be damned. Moreover worshippers of Mithras had none of the fierce, intolerant zeal possessed by Christians, and were quite willing to acknowledge the existence of other gods. Indeed statues of many different gods often shared a temple with Mithras. In the London temple the excavators found a fine head of Serapis, the Egyptian god of the harvest; a marble statuette of Mercury; a head of Minerva, goddess of wisdom; and a marble group representing Dionysus, the wine god, and his followers.

Mithraism, then, was a very tolerant religion, with none of the crusading zeal necessary to establish it as the state religion. Yet, of all the pagan religions, Mithraism was hated most by the rapidly growing numbers of Christians. You will perhaps have already noticed in the story of Mithras' life that there were some similarities between Mithraism and Christianity; Mithras like Jesus had a miraculous birth to which came shepherds bearing gifts, and like Jesus he partook of a last supper before ascending into heaven. In addition, worshippers of Mithras above the grade of Lion celebrated a ritual meal of bread and wine, which was compared with the Eucharist by horrified Christians; called Sunday the Day of the Lord; and kept December 25 as a holy day. Christians, as a result, regarded Mithraism as nothing but a devilish mockery of their own religion, and attacked it unrelentingly. When, in the fourth century, Christianity became the official religion of the Empire, the Mithraic temples were everywhere overthrown, and their sculptures whole-heartedly smashed. Christianity thus destroyed a hated rival.

From *The Story of Roman Britain*

26 A song to Mithras

RUDYARD KIPLING

In this poem, Rudyard Kipling imagines the kind of prayer sung
to Mithras.

Mithras, God of the Morning, our trumpets waken the Wall!
'Rome is above the Nations, but Thou art over all!'
Now as the names are answered, and the guards are marched away,
Mithras, also a soldier, give us strength for the day!

Mithras, God of the Noontide, the heather swims in the heat,
Our helmets scorch our foreheads; our sandals burn our feet.
Now in the ungirt hour; now lest we blink and drowse,
Mithras, also a soldier, keep us true to our vows!

Mithras, God of the Sunset, low on the Western main,
Thou descending immortal, immortal to rise again!
Now when the watch is ended, now when the wine is drawn,
Mithras, also a soldier, keep us pure till the dawn!

Mithras, God of the Midnight, here where the great bull dies,
Look on Thy children in darkness. Oh, take our sacrifice!
Many roads Thou hast fashioned: all of them lead to the Light!
Mithras, also a soldier, teach us to die aright!

From *Puck of Pook's Hill*

27   Stonehenge raid

G. SHIPWAY

The Romans were always tolerant of other religions, including, towards the end of the occupation, Christianity. But they never accepted the Druids because they constantly rallied their people against Rome. The following passage shows why one Roman soldier had other reasons for hating priests of the old religion.

One day we turned aside from the highway to visit a disused British temple on the plain near Old Sarum. I had heard much of this monument. The reality was somewhat disappointing because the great stones were dwarfed in the flat immensity of their surroundings. Nevertheless the concentric circles of hewn rock, encircled by bank and ditch, were not without grandeur. Melancholy and forlorn, they stood intact except for one of the tremendous inner portals, overthrown, as ancient digging showed, by human agency. I was unwillingly impressed despite a firm disbelief in gods and religion, Roman or barbarian.

'Does anyone know the history of this place?'

A man stirred in the bodyguard ranks.

'Permission to speak, Legate?'

'Your name?'

'Dossenius Proculus, centurion, seconded from II Legion Augusta.'

'Go on.'

'I was a recruit with the legion, under the legate Flavius Vespasianus, when we fought and conquered the southern tribes seventeen years ago. I accompanied a detachment sent to destroy this temple.'

I slid from my saddle and sat on a fallen stone, idly tracing with my finger some characters carved in a long-forgotten language.

'Tell me the story.'

'The legion was encamped at Winchester, which we had entered without resistance and found unoccupied. Cavalry were probing westwards, trying without success to find enemy. The countryside seemed deserted. We found later that many refugees had fled to the great Durotrigan fortress at Dorchester.

'One cavalry troop caught a Briton and brought him in for questioning. His story we only half understood: a garbled description of a war-band gathering at the Temple of the Sun. None of us had heard of this temple, then, or knew where it was. The legate decided investigation was worth while and detailed a cohort, with auxiliary infantry and cavalry, to destroy both war-band and temple, if it existed. We took the native as a guide.

'The place was a day's march distant, an unpleasant journey in freezing weather with a bitter wind howling under lowering clouds. We came to the plain and passed solitary huts, small settlements, round burial mounds. All were desolate, grey and lonely. In the afternoon it began snowing.

'We plodded on. The clouds descended, black and heavy. The snowfall turned to a blizzard. Visibility closed to a few yards; we lost sight of our cavalry, scouting at head and flanks. The tribune halted and closed the formation. Then our guide became reluctant, struggling and shouting. I put a javelin to his back and forced him on. We had no time to waste on remorseful traitors.

'Presently a cavalry scout reported something ahead: vast buildings, he said shakily, fires and hundreds of people. The guide was making a lot of noise, obviously trying to give warning. No one could have heard him beyond a javelin-cast in that gale, but he had done his job and was now a nuisance. We cut his throat.

'The tribune took me forward to the cavalry, halted in a fold of ground. We saw those monstrous stones and a great crowd filling the enclosure to the bank and beyond. Fires, whipped by the wind, sparked and flared within the inner horseshoe of lintelled pillars. The assembly was still, watching, intent upon something hidden from us behind the huge black rocks.

'Our preparations were short. Cavalry and auxiliaries moved silently to positions surrounding the temple. One century the tribune held in reserve; the other four formed line and drew swords. When all was ready the trumpets sounded.'

Proculus paused, rubbed his nose and coughed.

'I tell you this as it happened, Legate, believe me or not. In the snap of an eyelid the wind rose and hit us like a wave, screeching like a million demons. It was terrifying. The temple pillars, I swear, rocked before my eyes. The fires flicked out like candles. The crowd swayed; a crawling moan rose to an agonized shriek which drowned the gale.

'Well, the signal had been given. I was only a recruit, blinded by snow, wind-deaf and frightened. The veterans weren't feeling too sure of themselves, either, judging by the language. But it takes more than tempest to stop Valeria. We cleared the ditch at a run; our sword-points jarred on bone. After that it was all right. The first Britons died without knowing what killed them.

'The rest was panic and slaughter. We worked inwards from the circular bank, pushing the crowd together with our shields, shaving the outer edges with our blades like peeling layers from an onion. Women and children died with the rest; we had no orders about prisoners. There was practically no resistance until we reached the inner stone circle.

'Here, around these huge pillars, we had a proper fight. They made a tight ring, filling gaps between the stones with their bodies, fighting like men at the edge of hell. Within, above whooping trumpets, iron-clash and battle-yells, I heard men singing, high-voiced and despairing.

'It was soon over, and we were inside, where we are now: the inner sanctuary, I suppose you might call it. We found priests dressed in wolf skins, faces painted blue and yellow, bunched together, still chanting their death-song. The sight was so unexpected, unreal, that our men paused. Only then did I realize that the wind had dropped, suddenly and completely, and everything was still. The snow drifted down gently.'

Proculus kicked the stone on which he sat.

'This was an altar, Legate. Seventeen years ago two naked bodies lay on it, a boy and a girl. They were most delicately carved, like capons at a banquet. . . . Yet they still lived; their eyes moved; they knew.

'The tribune, a young fellow, saw and was sick. He was then angry and told us not to kill the priests. He put guards over them, and sent the auxiliaries hunting for timber, difficult enough to find in this treeless plain. They cut stakes, and we dug holes and planted the stakes five paces apart in a circle between the outermost stone ring and the bank. Then we bound the priests to the stakes, fifty-six in all, and stacked wood around them. It was full night by the time we finished.

'The wood was wet, green and burned badly, so that our torch-bearers were busy keeping the fires going. The priests died slowly, burning a little at a time, smouldering, moaning until the fires were rekindled, screaming when the flames leapt and bit. The horrors on the altar still lived and watched. None of us dared touch them.

'By morning all were dead. We worked all day to drag down the stones but they were heavy, the bases buried deep. We toppled only one of the portals. It lies there now.'

I rose stiffly. My fingers felt sticky where they had touched the stone; I bent and scrubbed them on the turf.

'Were these men Druids, Proculus?'

'As to that,' the centurion said, 'I cannot say, knowing nothing of barbarian customs. The tribune said they were not; he thought they were priests of an old religion, older than the Druids, as old as Britain itself.'

'Well, we have ended it.' I mounted and surveyed the stone circles, silent, brooding, evil. 'This place is accursed,' I added violently. 'Accursed and indestructible. If we cannot raze these pillars they must stand for ever. Yet two thousand empty years will not free their tormented ghosts. Let us go.'

The column swung across the plain. Dust rose beneath our feet, drifting in the sun behind the marching men, hiding the temple behind a dancing tapestry flecked with gold.

From *Imperial Governor*

28 Taliesin

JOHN JAMES

Others saw the Druids in a very different light. In this extract from *Not for all the Gold in Ireland*, a Greek merchant, Plotinus, and his Celtic friend Pryderi have been threatened by a hostile crowd at an inn, until their shabby travelling companion reveals himself as Taliesin the Druid.

Taliesin stood in the entrance. But not the Taliesin who had come with us, the ragged man in dirty brown, with muddy face and matted hair. Now he was wrapped in a robe of fine white linen that hid him from shoulder to foot, and I will swear that he had grown a head taller. His hair, red as Rhiannon's, was clean and combed and sleeked down with water. Upon his head he wore a wreath of oak leaves. The leaves were fresh, and the broken ends of the twigs were oozing sap, but the acorns, now in early August, were already hard and dry and brown-shelled and ripe. In his left hand, thrust from beneath his linen sheet, he held an apple, and in his right hand he held a sickle of the rich Gold of Ireland. And on his breast, held by a Golden pin, were a pair of bright green leaves and between them on the stem two fresh white berries. Whenever did you see the berries of the mistletoe ripe and smooth and plump in August?

It was late in the evening of a summer's day. It was still light enough to ride, but in the inn the servants had long lit the torches. The rain had stopped, but we could not see the setting sun for the low grey cloud. The air was misty. The whole land smelt of the warm steam. The birds were silent. Outside even the rooks and the pigeons of the wood had ceased to call.

In all that stillness, Taliesin the Druid walked through the filthy inn room. The floor was covered with straw littered with the bones and refuse of years of feasting. And I swear that I saw the straw move itself aside that his feet might touch only the sacred earth. The oak tables were stained with the spilt drink and gravy and littered with the fragments of the evening's dinners, and I saw the table legs bend back as the wood shrank lest Taliesin be defiled by the touch.

The old men in the room knelt before Taliesin, and the young men held their hands before their eyes that they might not be blinded by the radiance of his brow and the glory of his face, for they had not seen a Druid before in all their lives. He came to Rhiannon, and she went down on one knee before him, her skirts spread about her feet. She drew her shawl over her glorious hair, for respect, and the fringes of her shawl before her face, for modesty.

There stood Taliesin, walking as a Druid in a land where no Druid might walk abroad in freedom. He faced the rack and the cross and the fire, the lash and the salt mine and the beasts, and that for the sake—no, not for the sake of my life, nor of Pryderi's, nor for that of friendship in the abstract. He came for the sake of truth. Courage is a kind of holiness. I knelt before Taliesin.

From *Not for all the Gold in Ireland*

29 Out of the rain

JOHN JAMES

There must have been many features of the Britons' way of life
that Romans never really knew. Here the Greek merchant of the
last passage takes refuge in a small native inn, a place probably never
entered by any Roman.

We stopped eventually outside an inn, and this at last was a real
Brits' stopping place. The other inns where we had slept had all been
possible, just possible stopping places for civilized men who weren't
too particular, but this was no place for anyone who was not native
born. We had stopped in the middle of the day for a bite of cold
roast venison and an oatcake we bought from a girl at a farmhouse
by the way. All alone she was, and baking like a mad thing, for
every other soul was in the fields at the last of the wheat harvest.

I remarked that I had already tasted enough of that stag to see me
through a lifetime. Pryderi laughed.

'And it's more of him you'll be having for your supper, but it's
depending I am on him to pay for our beds too.'

Sure enough, he was just able to persuade the innkeeper that it
would be just to take the carcase of the deer, and the hide and horns,
to pay our bill.

Now, this was the first British house I had stayed in, that is to
say, the first built in the British way. For all the nations of the earth
build their houses with straight walls, and it is only the houses of
their gods and their graves that they make round. But your Brit
likes to build himself a round house, and simple it is to do. First of
all you mark out a circle on the ground, and around this circle you
dig holes two or three paces apart. In each hole you set an upright
post, twice the height of a man. Then you join the timbers together
with light rafters, and this you can thatch, leaving a hole in the

middle of the roof for the smoke of the fire. Perhaps the house is not big enough for you. All right, then draw another circle outside the first, and set there another ring of uprights, and thatch the roof between the inner and outer rings, and if you feel so inclined there is always room for another circle, because you have all the island to cover if you have a mind to. The walls you then fill in with basketwork caulked with mud, or even with a few courses of stone. If for any reason you are not satisfied with one open hall to live in, then you can join uprights together to make booths, and so this inn consisted of a great round house, with an open hall at the door, and a ring of booths at the farther circumference.

We exchanged our deer, then, for the use of a booth for a night, and glad we were to get into it, because the luck that had brought us dry, if not fine, weather now deserted us. The cloud got lower as the morning wore on. The girl who sold us the oatcake was looking anxiously at the first few drops showing on the flagstone at her door, and awaiting the rush home from the fields. By the time we reached the inn, three hours after noon, the rain was falling steadily in a monotonous drizzle, not heavily, but thoroughly. I was tolerably dry myself, because I put on my seal-skin cloak, and that shed water like—well, have you ever seen a seal? The other two had their soft leather jerkins, but all the same we were glad to get indoors.

From *Not for all the Gold in Ireland*

30 On the run

ALFRED DUGGAN

If Romans did not enter village inns, it is unlikely that a chief administrator of Britain would choose to sleep in a British hut—unless for some reason he was on the run!

He was brought back to the present by the crashing of some large animal in the bushes near at hand. He had often heard, whenever he planned to celebrate Games for the honour of the government, that there were no dangerous beasts in southern Britain; but it was hard to believe that now, when something with a thick skin that did not feel the thorns was blundering nearer and nearer; he sprang to his feet, his iron-shod staff held aloft. Then the beast made a snuffling noise, and even Felix the city-dweller recognized it for a hog. This was something he had not bargained for; he knew sheep were folded at night, and he had assumed that other animals were shut up also. But this was a valuable creature, and the swineherd would not be far off.

Sure enough, there was something else pushing through the scrub, and then a voice called. But it was the voice of a young girl. He made up his mind almost without conscious thought. He was armed, and could silence her if she called for help; but if she was friendly she could lead him to food, and he wanted food more than anything in the world, more even than safety. He forced his way in the direction of the voice, driving the pig before him.

A faint light seeped through the clouds; the pig was a moving shadow against the black ground, and then he made out the girl standing in an open glade. Presumably the pig had strayed; it was comforting to know that the countryside was so peaceful that a small girl could be sent to search for it in the dark. Then the child was aware of a stranger; she called out in the local dialect, and ran back a few steps. But she was not so frightened as to run away and abandon the pig; she halted until he drew nearer, then took to her heels again; and in this manner they approached a cottage standing alone in the scrub.

An isolated cottage was just the place to get supplies; if the inhabitants proved unfriendly he could kill them with his sword, for coloni were forbidden to possess arms. But if he kept silent, and they did not guess who he was, they might help him willingly. The girl scuttled through the low entrance on hands and knees, followed by the pig. Felix halted beside the dark mass of the hut, whose thatched roof reached in one sweep to within a foot of the ground; to enter he must go down on his hands, and the householder could crack his head before he had a chance to draw his sword. But he felt keyed up to run risks, and at that moment he smelled grilling bacon, the most entrancing odour that can reach a starving man. He wallowed through the low entry with his knees stumbling over his trailing cloak, and sat back on his haunches, his right hand feeling for the sword under his arm.

The hut seemed bigger from within. Dry sticks had been laid on the ashes of the central hearth, and small flames were beginning to creep round them, for it was nearly morning; through the smoke he could see an old woman holding a skewer over the flame, with the delicious bacon sizzling on it, and behind her several pigs lay in a heap; to one side a mound of rushes suddenly erupted, and the man of the house crouched on his knees, with his head brushing the slope of the thatch and a billhook in his hand. He shouted, and glared fiercely. Felix, dazed with fatigue, acted on the inspiration of the moment; he pulled out his sword, laid it beside the hearth, and squatted with empty hands on his lap. It was the classic attitude of a suppliant, which old-fashioned country people should understand.

The householder understood; with a deliberate ritual movement he placed the billhook across the sword, though he left the handle towards him, and if it came to a scuffle he would reach his weapon first. Then he repeated his question. Felix shook his head, and spoke a few words of Libyan that he remembered from his childhood. This visit would pass off more pleasantly if his hosts could not converse with him. He grinned at the man, then at the woman, and finally at the girl, whose head, with two other tousled little heads, now appeared from the tangle of pigs at the back of the hut; then he pointed at his mouth, to show he was hungry.

Peasants do not turn away a starving man, but he would get better food from this hovel if he offered to pay. Yet he thought it unsafe to show his gold. Was there anything he could offer instead? He needed his weapons and his cloak; but his brogues were well made, though it would be weeks before he could put them on his raw and swollen feet. He scrambled over to the old woman, put the shoes in her lap, and took the skewer with its lump of bacon out of her hand; then he looked to the man, to see if he approved.

That was enough to make them all intimate friends. For the next hour, though he stuffed himself with bacon and barley scones, Felix had rather a trying time. He was desperately sleepy, but the others were just waking up, and they were convinced that if only they shouted loud enough they could get him to understand Celtic. Under his cloak he still wore the fine linen tunic that he had put on two days ago; the peasants noticed it with puzzled admiration. A runaway slave would not possess such a garment. Presently they decided he must be a fugitive baker, in his best clothes; for the old woman (she looked much older than her husband, but then she probably worked harder) made cooking motions at the fire and waved a lump of dough, while the man laughed and thumped him on the back. The baker was the stock example of a skilled craftsman held to unremunerative forced labour, all over the Roman world; it was the only city trade these primitive swineherds could imagine.

The woman tried on the shoes and liked them; to show her goodwill she rummaged among the pigs and children at the back of the hut and brought out a small jug of barley drink; but Felix refused it, for he guessed it would make him sick; and anyway this was no time for drinking, with the sun just rising.

But all this friendliness in pantomime had given him an idea; if he could make them understand, these new allies might lead him to a boat. He went through the motions of paddling, and pointed southward in the direction of the river. At first his hosts were merely amused at his actions, but presently they grasped what he was trying to convey, and there was a short argument between husband and wife; it seemed that she had some plan, which he considered too dangerous or too difficult. But it was time to let out the pigs; they could not talk round the fire in broad daylight. The man made up his mind with a sudden gesture of decision, and crawled out of the hut; his wife and the two small children gathered the cooking pots into a little heap, which they guarded as the girl drove out the swine; Felix also crawled through the thick pig-dung which daylight revealed in the entry, and waited outside for the next move. His light slippers were wet through and caked with greasy dung; they would be quite useless on the march. He must have a boat.

The swineherd stood jabbering in great excitement. He was trying to explain something, but of course he had never met anyone who did not speak Celtic; he found it very difficult to remember that even shouting was no use. His wife was more intelligent. She was wearing the brogues that had paid for breakfast; now she took them off, gave them for a moment to Felix, snatched them back and held out her hand for more; then she made the motion of paddling. Plainly there was a boat, but he must pay for it.

Once that was understood negotiations did not take long. Felix brought out the few silver coins that even a poor fugitive might possess, and held them on the palm of his hand; they should be enough, and anyway he dared not show his gold; ten solidi were a fortune, for which the peasants might be tempted to murder him. But these people were not only poor, they were honest. The man took less than half the silver, and set off south-west down a winding overgrown trail. Felix followed, after grinning good-bye to the rest of the family; a moment later he was overtaken by a small urchin carrying his sword, which he had forgotten, and a little bag of oatmeal. They were really a very nice family, in spite of their barbarous manner of life.

Through the bushes they caught a glimpse of the roofs of Pontes, and went cautiously; but after a couple of miles they reached the river. It was swollen with autumn rains, flowing through a maze of swampy channels. Hidden among rushes were a dug-out canoe and a round leather coracle. Both had evidently carried pigs since last they were cleaned, but the canoe was fit for a long journey; though it was hollowed from a single tree the sides had been built up with inter-laced willows and clay. Presumably the coracle was used to take animals to market, and the canoe to chase any adventurous pig who went for a swim. The swineherd took a paddle from the fork of a nearby tree, laid it on the ground, and walked steadily away without looking back. From his experience in the law courts Felix understood; the man would have to swear before his master that the boat had been stolen in his absence, and he did not wish to offend the gods by perjury.

From *The Little Emperors*

Following on

1 Imagine that you are a young and very keen Roman officer, posted for duty on the Wall. Describe your first day there as you encounter various officers and men who do not come up to the standards you expect.

2 Write a similar account of the young officer's first day by a hardened old veteran of the Wall. Give his version of how a man should behave in such circumstances and his attitude to the young Roman who has just arrived.

3 Imagine that you are a veteran Pict warrior talking about the Wall to the young men of his tribe. You could include descriptions of how the Romans first built the Wall, of various attacks upon it, and the ways in which the Wall became an important part of life for the Picts. In writing this you might find *Puck of Pook's Hill* by Rudyard Kipling useful.

4 Describe an interview between the Roman administrator in 'The problems of peace' and a local landowner who wants a favour from him. Remember what sort of man the administrator is, and also what power he has.

5 Write an essay about the Druids, giving both sides of the picture. Remember their cruelty, but also their importance to their followers.

6 From what you have gathered in the extracts, describe the ordinary life and dwellings of the common British people.

7 Imagine that the British family who had sheltered the fleeing Roman official were in due course interrogated by Roman soldiers who were hunting him down. Describe what happened.

The Romans leave

31 The Roman centurion's song

RUDYARD KIPLING

In the fifth century the Roman occupation of Britain was coming to
an end as troops were withdrawn to fight on the Continent. In this
poem, a Roman officer shows his agony at having to leave the land he
has served and come to love.

Legate, I had the news last night—my cohort ordered home
By ship to Portus Itius and thence by road to Rome.
I've marched the companies aboard, the arms are stowed below:
Now let another take my sword. Command me not to go!

I've served in Britain forty years, from Vectis to the Wall.
I have none other home than this, nor any life at all.
Last night I did not understand, but, now the hour draws near
That calls me to my native land, I feel that land is here.

Here where men say my name was made, here where my work was
      done;
Here where my dearest dead are laid—my wife—my wife and son;
Here where time, custom, grief and toil, age, memory, service, love,
Have rooted me in British soil. Ah, how can I remove?

For me this land, that sea, these airs, those folk and fields suffice.
What purple Southern pomp can match our changeful Northern
      skies,
Black with December snows unshed or pearled with August haze—
The clanging arch of steel-grey March, or June's long-lighted days?

You'll follow widening Rhodanus till vine and olive lean
Aslant before the sunny breeze that sweeps Nemausus clean
To Arelate's triple gate; but let me linger on,
Here where our stiff-necked British oaks confront Euroclydon!

You'll take the old Aurelian road through shore-descending pines
Where, blue as a peacock's neck, the Tyrrhene Ocean shines.
You'll go where laurel crowns are won, but—will you e'er forget
The scent of hawthorn in the sun, or bracken in the wet?

Let me work here for Britain's sake—at any task you will—
A marsh to drain, a road to make or native troops to drill.
Some Western camp (I know the Pict) or granite Border keep,
Mid seas of heather derelict, where our old messmates sleep.

Legate, I come to you in tears—My cohort ordered home!
I've served in Britain forty years. What should I do in Rome?
Here is my heart, my soul, my mind—the only life I know.
I cannot leave it all behind. Command me not to go!

From *Puck of Pook's Hill*

32 The Romans leave

BEDE

Some 400 years after conquering Britain, Rome, its Empire under attack nearer home, began to withdraw from its northernmost province. In the following passage, the great eighth century recorder, Bede, recalls how the descendants of the people who had fought their coming now begged the Roman legions not to go.

Rome fell to the Goths in the 1164th year after its foundation. At the same time Roman rule came to an end in Britain, almost 470 years after the landing of Gaius Julius Caesar. The Romans had occupied the country south of the earthwork which, as I have said, Severus built across the island (in AD 189), as cities, forts, bridges, and paved roads bear witness to this day: they also held nominal jurisdiction over the more remote parts of Britain and the islands beyond it.

Henceforward, the part of Britain inhabited by the Britons which had been hurriedly stripped of all troops and military equipment and robbed of the flower of its young men, who had been led away by ambitious despots and were never to return, lay wholly exposed to attack, since its people were untrained in the science of war. Consequently for many years this region suffered attacks from two savage extraneous races, Scots from the northwest, and Picts from the north. I term these races extraneous, not because they came from outside Britain, but because their lands were sundered from that of the Britons: for two sea estuaries lay between, one of which runs broad and deep into the country from the sea to the east and the other from the west, although they do not actually meet. In the middle of the eastern estuary stands the city of Giudi (the island of Inchkeith), while on the right bank of the western stands the city of Alcluith (Dumbarton), which in their language means 'the rock of Cluith', as it stands near a river of that name.

When these tribes invaded them, the Britons sent messengers to Rome with moving appeals for help, promising perpetual submission if only the Romans would drive out their enemies. An armed legion was quickly dispatched to the island, where it engaged the enemy, inflicted heavy losses on them, and drove the survivors out of the territory of Rome's allies. Having thus freed the Britons for a time from dire oppression, the Romans advised them to construct a protective wall across the island from sea to sea in order to keep their foes at bay. The victorious Legion then returned home. The islanders built this wall as they had been instructed, but having no engineers capable of so great an undertaking, they built it of turf and not of stone, so that it was of small value. However, they built it for many miles between the two above-mentioned estuaries or inlets, hoping that where the sea provided no protection, they might use the rampart to preserve their borders from hostile attack. Clear traces of this wide and lofty earthwork can be seen to this day. It begins about two miles west of the monastery of Aebbercurnig (Abercorn) at a place which the Picts call Peanfahel and the English Penneltun (Old Kilpatrick), and runs westward to the vicinity of the city of Alcluith. But as soon as the old enemies of the Britons saw that the Roman forces had left, they made a seaborne invasion, breaking in and destroying wholesale, slaughtering right and left as men cut ripe corn. The Britons therefore sent more envoys to Rome with pitiful appeals for help, without which their unhappy land would be utterly ravaged and the name of a once illustrious Roman province be brought into disgrace and obliterated by barbarous tribes, who year by year were carrying off their plunder unchecked. Once more a Legion was dispatched, which arrived unexpectedly in autumn and inflicted heavy casualties on the invaders, forcing all who survived to escape by sea.

The Romans, however, now informed the Britons that they could no longer undertake such troublesome expeditions for their defence, and urged them to take up arms for their own part and cultivate the will to fight, pointing out that it was solely their lack of spirit which gave their enemies an advantage over them. In addition, in order to assist these allies whom they were forced to abandon, they built a strong wall of stone directly from sea to sea in a straight line between the towns that had been built as strong-points, where

Severus had built his earthwork. This famous and still conspicuous wall was built from public and private resources, with the Britons lending assistance. It is eight feet in breadth and twelve in height; and, as can be clearly seen to this day, ran straight from east to west. When the wall was completed, the Romans gave firm advice to the dispirited Britons, together with instructions on the manufacture of weapons. In addition, they built towers at intervals overlooking the south coast where their ships lay, because there was a danger of barbarian raids even from this quarter. Then they bade farewell to their allies, with no intention of ever returning.

On the departure of the Romans, the Picts and Scots, learning that they did not mean to return, were quick to return themselves, and becoming bolder than ever, occupied all the northern and outer part of the island up to the wall, as if it belonged to them. Here a dispirited British garrison stationed on the fortifications pined in terror night and day, while from beyond the wall the enemy constantly harassed them with hooked weapons, dragging the cowardly defenders down from their wall and dashing them to the ground. At length the Britons abandoned their cities and wall and fled in disorder, pursued by their foes. The slaughter was more ghastly than ever before, and the wretched citizens were torn in pieces by their enemies, as lambs are torn by wild beasts. They were driven from their homesteads and farms, and sought to save themselves from starvation by robbery and violence against one another, their own internal anarchy adding to the miseries caused by others, until there was no food left in the whole land except whatever could be obtained by hunting.

From *A History of the English Church and People* transl. L. Sherley-Price

33   The last beacon

ROSEMARY SUTCLIFF

Not all the Romans left Britain. In this extract from *The Lantern Bearers* by Rosemary Sutcliff, one young officer is determined to stay, and lights the great warning beacon against the oncoming darkness.

And now the last feverish hours of getting the horses into the transports were over, and the men had been marched aboard while the brazen orders of the trumpets rang above the ordered tumult; and there was scarcely anything more to do. A flamed and feathered sunset was fading behind the Great Forest, and the tide was almost at the flood, running far up the creeks and inlets and winding waterways; and amid the last ordered coming and going, Aquila stood on the lifting deck of the *Clytemnestra*. The stern and mast-head lantern were alight already, as the daylight dimmed, and any moment now the great fire-beacon on the crest of the Pharos should have sprung to life. But there would be no Rutupiae Light tonight to guide the fleets of the Empire. The last of the Eagles were flying from Britain. Any moment now the trumpets would sound as the Commandant came down from the Watergate and stepped on board, and the landing-bridge would be raised, and the Hortator's hammer would begin the steady, remorseless clack-clack-clack that beat out the time for the slaves on the rowing benches.

Aquila suddenly saw himself going to the Commandant in that last moment, laying his drawn sword at his feet, saying, 'Sir, everything is in order. Now let me go.' Would Callistus think that he was mad or hysterical? No, oddly enough—for there had never been a word between them save in the way of duty—he knew that Callistus would understand; but he knew also that Callistus would have no choice but to refuse. The choice was his. Quite clearly and coldly, in the still moment after the three days' turmoil, he knew that he must make it alone.

He turned to his old, grey-whiskered optio beside him, who had taught him all that he knew of soldiering, all that he knew of the handling of a troop—he had been so proud of his troop—and gripped his leather-clad shoulder an instant.

'God keep you, Aemilius. I'll be back.'

He turned to the head of the landing-bridge and crossed over, quickly and openly as though in obedience to some last-moment order. No chance to bid good-bye to Felix, none to take leave of Nestor, his horse. He strode by the last remaining figures on the jetty, the native dockyard hands, no one particularly noticing him in the fading light, back through the Watergate into the desolate fort.

Everything in him felt bruised and bleeding. He had been bred a soldier, coming of a line of soldiers, and he was breaking faith with all the gods of his kind. Going 'wilful missing'. The very words had the sorry sound of disgrace. He was failing the men of his own troop, which seemed to him in that moment a worse thing than all else. Yet he did not turn back again to the waiting galleys. He knew that what he was doing was a thing that you couldn't judge for other people, only for yourself; and for himself, he did not know if it was the right thing, but he knew that it was the only thing.

He was scarcely aware of his direction, until he found himself at the foot of the Pharos. The ramp for the fuel-carts led steeply upwards to the vast plinth, and at the head of it the mouth of the covered way gaped dark and empty in the gathering dusk. He mounted the ramp quickly and strode forward into the darkness. He was in the square hollowness of the tower foot where the fuel-carts were housed. The carts were there now, ranged side by side, mere blots of darkness in the lesser darkness. The dry, musty smell of baled straw was in his nostrils, and the sharp tang of pitch that had soaked into the stones of the walls. He turned to the narrow staircase that wound up the wall like the spiral twist of a snail shell, and began to climb.

He was only half-way up when he heard, faintly through the thick walls from the world outside, the trumpets sounding the Commandant on board. Any moment now he would be missed. Well, they would have little time for searching. They would not miss the tide for one junior officer gone wilful missing. He climbed on, up and up, stumbling a little, through chamber after chamber,

H

with the sense of height increasing upon him, past the deserted quarters where the men on beacon duty had lived like peregrine falcons high above the world. The grey dusk seeping through the small windows showed the dark shapes of the debris they had left behind them—rough wooden furniture and cast-off gear, like the stranded flotsam on the shore left when the tide flows out, as Rome's tide was flowing out. Up and up until the stairway ran out into the open air, and he ducked at last through a little low-set door-way into complete darkness, into the 'Immediate Use' fuel store just below the signal platform. Feeling with outstretched hands, he found the ranged barrels of pitch, the straw and brushwood and stacked logs. A gap opened to his questing hand between the brushwood and the wall, and he crawled into it and crouched there, pulling the brushwood over again behind him.

It wasn't a good hiding-place, but the tide would be already on the turn.

For what seemed a very long time he crouched there, his heart beating in slow, uneven drubs. From far, far below him, in another world, he thought he heard the tramp of mailed sandals and voices that shouted his name. He wondered what he should do if they came up here and found him, skulking like a cornered rat under a garbage pile; but the time passed, and the footsteps and the calling voices came and went, hurrying, but never mounted the stairs of the forsaken tower. And presently the trumpets sounded again, recalling the searchers lest they lose the tide. Too late now to change his mind.

More time passed and he knew that the galleys would be slipping down the broad river-way between the marshes. And then once more he heard the trumpets. No, only one. The call was faint, faint as the echo of a seabird's cry; but Aquila's ear caught the sad, familiar notes of the call. In one of those galleys slipping seaward, somebody, in savage comment on what had happened, or merely in farewell, was sounding 'Lights Out'.

And now that it was all over, now that the choice was made, and one faith kept and one faith broken, Aquila drove his face down on his forearm against the whippy roughness of the brushwood bundles, and cried as he had never cried before and would never cry again.

A long while later he turned himself about in his hiding-place, and ducked out on to the narrow stairway, spent and empty as though he had cried his heart away. Dusk had long since deepened into the dark, and the cold moonlight came down the steps from the beacon platform, plashing silvery from step to step. And as he checked there, leaning against the wall, the silence of the great fortress came up to him, a silence of desolation and complete emptiness. On a sudden impulse he turned upward towards the moonlight instead of down into the blackness that swallowed the descending stairway, and stumbled up the last few steps, emerging on the beacon platform.

The moon was riding high in a sky pearled and feathered with high wind-cloud, and a little wind sighed across the breast-high parapet with a faint aeolian hum through the iron-work of the beacon tripod. The brazier was made up ready for lighting, with fuel stacked beside it, as it had been stacked every night. Aquila crossed to the parapet and stood looking down. There were lights in the little ragged town that huddled against the fortress walls, but the great fort below him was empty and still in the moonlight as a ruin that had been hearth-cold for a hundred years. Presently, in the daylight, men would come and strip the place of whatever was useful to them, but probably after dark they would leave it forsaken and empty to its ghosts. Would they be the ghosts of the men who had sailed on this tide? Or of the men who had left their names on the leaning gravestones above the wash of the tide? A Cohort Centurion with a Syrian name, dying after thirty years' service, a boy trumpeter of the Second Legion, dying after two. . . .

Aquila's gaze lengthened out across the marshes in the wake of the galleys, and far out to sea he thought that he could still make out a spark of light. The stern lantern of a transport; the last of Rome-in-Britain. And beside him the beacon stack rose dark and waiting. . . . On a sudden wild impulse he flung open the bronze-sheathed chest in which the fire-lighting gear was kept, and pulled out flint and steel and tinderbox, and tearing his fingers on the steel in his frantic haste, as though he were fighting against time, he struck out fire and kindled the waiting tinder, and set about waking the beacon. Rutupiae Light should burn for this one more night. Maybe Felix or his old optio would know who had kindled it, but that was not what mattered. The pitch-soaked brushwood caught, and the flames ran crackling up, spreading into a great golden burst of fire; and the still, moonlit world below faded into a blue nothingness as the fierce glare flooded the beacon platform. The wind caught the crest of the blaze and bent it over in a wave; and Aquila's shadow streamed out from him across the parapet and into

107

the night like a ragged cloak. He flung water from the tank in the corner on the blackened bull's-hide fire-shield, and crouched holding it before him by the brazier, feeding the blaze to its greatest strength. The heart of it was glowing now, a blasting, blinding core of heat and brightness under the flames; even from the shores of Gaul they would see the blaze, and say, 'Ah, there is Rutupiae's Light.' It was his farewell to so many things; to the whole world that he had been bred to. But it was something more: a defiance against the dark.

He vaguely half-expected them to come up from the town to see who had lit the beacon, but no one came. Perhaps they thought it was the ghosts. Presently he stoked it up so that it would last for a while, and turned to the stairhead and went clattering down. The beacon would sink low, but he did not think it would go out much before dawn.

He reached the ground level; the moonlight hung like a silver curtain before the doorway, and he walked out into it and across the deserted fortress, and out through a postern gate that stood open, and away. He had the sudden thought that for the sake of the fitness of things he should have broken his sword across his knee and left the pieces beside Rutupiae Light, but he was like to need it in the time that lay ahead.

From *The Lantern Bearers*

34   On Wenlock Edge

A. E. HOUSMAN

The legions left but all over the country signs of Roman settlement remain, reminding us of our links with a great people. Uricon was a Roman settlement on the Anglo–Welsh border, the present-day Wroxeter.

On Wenlock Edge the wood's in trouble;
   His forest fleece the Wrekin heaves;
The gale, it plies the saplings double,
   And thick on Severn snow the leaves.

'Twould blow like this through holt and hanger
   When Uricon the city stood;
'Tis the old wind in the old anger,
   But then it threshed another wood.

Then, 'twas before my time, the Roman
   At yonder heaving hill would stare:
The blood that warms an English yeoman,
   The thoughts that hurt him, they were there.

There, like the wind through woods in riot,
   Through him the gale of life blew high;
The tree of man was never quiet:
   Then 'twas the Roman, now 'tis I.

The gale, it plies the saplings double,
   It blows so hard, 'twill soon be gone:
Today the Roman and his trouble
   Are ashes under Uricon.

From *Collected Poems*

Following on

1 Imagine the fears of the people left behind when the Romans finally departed. Write a scene for a play in which a number of landowners and wealthy men beg the local Roman commander to stay behind and protect them.

2 Describe the scene in the first few days after the Romans have gone. What precautions would have to be taken; and what quarrelling would go on in deciding them?

3 Continue the episode from *The Lantern Bearers*, showing what happened to Aquila immediately after the last legions had left. What would he do? Where would he go?

4 Describe a scene in which invaders from the sea make their first attack on the now unprotected land.

5 Imagine what Aquila would do to rally the people to protect themselves. Describe the scene where he announces himself and is chosen to be their leader.

6 Imagine what Aquila might be doing ten years after the departure of the legions. Write an account of a day in his life at this time.

Dates

212	All free provincials allowed Roman citizenship.
275–87	Saxon pirates become a threat in the Channel.
296	Barbarians attack in the North.
313	Christianity allowed.
360	Raids in the North by Picts and Scots, culminating in the great invasion of 367 by these tribes and their allies, Attacotti and Saxon pirates.
361	St Alban martyred at Verulamium (St Albans).
369	Theodosius is sent from Rome to clear Britain of invaders and to rebuild the Wall.
383	Hadrian's Wall is swamped by invaders and is not rebuilt.
406	The Roman legions leave Britain as the usurping Emperor Constantine III strips Britain of its troops for his conquest of Gaul and Spain.
410	The people of Britain are told to arrange their own defence.
c.446	The last appeal to Rome for help.

Bibliography

1 Dewey numbers which should be of use

878   Miscellaneous Latin literature, journals and prose works
913.42 Archaeology in the British Isles
937   Roman history
942   General history of the British Isles
942.01 History of the British Isles up to AD 1066.
Books on such specialist topics as the Roman army, Roman roads, Roman buildings, etc., may appear under other numbers in the Dewey Classification.

2 Seeing Roman Britain: maps, museums, sites and books

The Ordnance Survey Map of Roman Britain (3rd ed.) H.M.S.O., 1956
This is far more than a map. A detailed chronological table of Roman Britain and a complete index of Roman place names and their modern equivalents are clearly set out, together with detailed maps of small areas to show the extent and nature of the Roman occupation. Ptolemy's map of Britain is printed, and makes a striking contrast with the large coloured map showing our present state of knowledge about Roman Britain. Symbols show everything from salt-boiling sites to signal stations and from practice camps to lighthouses. This excellent publication can be a source of delightful information-seeking for anyone. It is probably the most valuable aid of all to this volume.

Museums and sites
The Ordnance Survey Map of Roman Britain will show the whereabouts of any local Roman sites. Some of these may be the subject

of pamphlets published for the Ministry of Works by H.M.S.O., which publishes a sectional list, *Ancient Monuments and Historic Buildings*. These pamphlets are available from any bookseller or from H.M.S.O. by post.

The Ministry of Works maintains several Roman sites, and many towns and cities are proud of their Roman remains. Some of these are well worth visiting. Many museums have Roman exhibits and may well welcome school visits if they are arranged beforehand. The Museum of Antiquities at Newcastle-upon-Tyne, for example, can make arrangements for party visits. Like several other museums, it has a range of books, postcards and colour slides for sale, at the museum or by post. The selection from this particular museum is particularly large and contains much about Hadrian's Wall. Fuller details may be obtained from The Keeper and Secretary, The Museum of Antiquities, The Quadrangle, The University, Newcastle-upon-Tyne, NE1 7RU.

The Archaeology of Roman Britain
R. Collingwood and I. Richmond, Methuen, 1969
This is the basic book for any work on this topic. It is well worth consulting, and many teachers should find it of particular help and interest.

Seeing Roman Britain
L. Cottrell, Evans Brothers, 1957
Mr Cottrell takes his reader on a tour of what remains of Roman Britain, showing his excellent knowledge and his flair for imaginative reconstruction. He splits the book into sections dealing with particular towns and areas, so that a teacher can quickly find out about his own locality. The book is valuable for its chronological table, its list of Roman place names and the modern equivalents, and a list of relevant museums.

A Guide to the Prehistoric and Roman Monuments in England and Wales
J. Hawkes, Chatto and Windus, 1957
This is another book for the teacher. Miss Hawkes writes of 'nearly all the prehistoric and Roman antiquities of England and Wales which the eye and the imagination can still enjoy, and gives some account of their history'. The country is dealt with in areas, so that

114

the teacher in a hurry can find out about his own locality quite quickly. There is a helpful twenty-three page gazetteer at the back of the book.

Roman Roads in Britain
I. Margary, John Baker, revised ed., 1967
This revised edition of the classic work on Roman roads in Britain is the most complete account of its kind. Britain is divided into ten areas, thus making it easy for the teacher to find out about local roads. The book has excellent maps and some very fine photographs.

Collins Field Guide to Archaeology in Britain
E. Wood, Collins, 1963
This field guide deals with the whole range of archaeology in Britain, but it is well indexed and it is easy to find the sections on Roman remains. The book is very fully illustrated with photographs and line drawings. Teachers may find it useful, and it may well interest pupils who find themselves drawn to the topic of Roman Britain.

3   Contemporary and early accounts of Roman Britain

A History of the English Church and People
Bede, transl. L. Sherley-Price, Penguin, 1968 (revised ed.)
Much of the early part of this famous early history of Britain is on the subject. It is simply written and may well appeal to the enthusiastic pupil as well as to teachers. Bede is particularly valuable for his account of the later years of Roman Britain and the events after the Romans left.

The Conquest of Gaul
Julius Caesar, transl. S. A. Handford, Penguin, 1951
Caesar wrote his own account of his two expeditions to Britain. This book shows the austere and disciplined mind of a great Roman soldier and tells the readers something about the people who resisted him. It also shows that Britain was not the only province of Rome, and that other parts of Europe also occupied Rome's attention!

The History of the Kings of Britain
Geoffrey of Monmouth, transl. L. Thorpe, Penguin, 1966
This is a fascinating mixture of history and legend. It was written

about AD 1136 and is an account of some nineteen centuries of British history, some of which is not entirely reliable! It is a pageant of famous names (Leir, Cymbeline, the Arthurian legend) and ranges in its material from an account of the unfortunate King Bladud who tried to fly in 815 BC and crashlanded on the temple of Apollo, to the comment that the Britons called Caesar's sword 'Yellow Death'.

On Britain and Germany
P. Cornelius Tacitus, transl. H. Mattingly, Penguin, 1948
Two works are in this volume—the 'Agricola' and the 'Germania' of Tacitus—but it is the first which is relevant. It is a clear and simple account of the work and campaigns in Britain of its most famous Roman governor, Julius Agricola. This and Caesar's account of his contact with Britain may appeal to some pupils as well as to teachers.

4   The history of Roman Britain

The Story of Roman Britain
D. R. Barker, Edward Arnold, 1963
This is a very good background book for pupils to use. The author has written a series of reconstructions of military and civilian life and uses these to convey a great amount of factual information. The book is clearly written and well illustrated.

Life in Roman Britain
A. Birley, Batsford, 1964
Mr Birley has written an excellent basic book for the teacher and one which many children could also enjoy. The book is written in a clear and lively manner, and its illustrations are very well produced.

Celtic Britain
N. Chadwick, Thames and Hudson, 1964 (revised ed.)
This book is something of an outsider, but some teachers may find it interesting. It shows to what extent and in what ways Celtic life had continued unbroken throughout the Roman period of British history and how its culture emerged once more when the Romans left. The book is notable for its illustrations.

The Great Invasion
L. Cottrell, Evans Brothers, 1958; Pan Books, 1961
Mr Cottrell's book deals with the invasion of Britain from the first
expedition of Caesar to the Caledonian campaign of Agricola. It is
a lively and imaginative work, and many pupils will enjoy it as much
as their teachers. The book is well illustrated.

The Roman Conquest of Britain
R. Dudley and G. Webster, Batsford, 1965
The authors of this well illustrated study have written an excellent
account of the invasion of AD 43. Contemporary accounts are used
in a book notable for its elegant style and scholarship. Many teachers
may find this book interesting, and may like to read *The Rebellion
of Boudicca* by the same authors, published by Routledge and Kegan
Paul, 1963.

Britain, Rome's Most Northerly Province
G. M. Durant, Bell, 1969
This recent history is written in an attractive and lively style, and
is an excellent blend of enthusiasm and scholarship. It is a particularly good background book for teachers, and some children may
well like to tackle it.

Roman Britain
A. Fox and A. Sorrell, Lutterworth Press, 1961
This is a splendid book. The text by Lady Fox is brief and com-
mendably clear. Mr Sorrell's series of large drawings of scenes in
Roman Britain are notable for their scholarship and sense of being
alive; they are bound to excite lots of discussion and further work.
This book should be on the library shelves.

The next two books are large, expensive and beautifully produced,
and are probably the most comprehensive works on Roman Britain
that are available. They are certainly worth obtaining from the
local library even if your own school cannot afford them.

Britannia—A History of Roman Britain
Professor S. Frere, Routledge & Kegan Paul, 1967
This book starts its discussion of Roman Britain in pre-Roman times.
It is a large and rewarding work for any interested teacher, and it is

notable for its comprehensiveness and for its use of recent discoveries and scholarship. The whole book is beautifully printed, and the large format adds to the impact of the fine appendix of photographs.

Britain in the Roman Empire
J. Liversidge, Routledge & Kegan Paul, 1968
Miss Liversidge has written an erudite and fascinating work. Again, it is one for the teacher to read and convey to the class. It explores all aspects of life in Roman Britain, ranging from the well-known to such oddities as the fact that hairdressers studied new coins to see the latest hairstyle of the Empress! The book is very well illustrated, and many of the line drawings and diagrams could be the source of very good wall-charts. The book is particularly valuable because it deals mainly with civilian life, an aspect of Roman Britain which can easily be ignored.

Everyday Life in Roman and Anglo-Saxon Times
M. and C. H. B. Quennell, Batsford, 1960
This is a very good book for any topic work on Roman Britain. Pupils will find it valuable for its extensive line illustrations of life at that time and in particular for those dealing with objects and how they were used.

Roman Britain
I. A. Richmond, Penguin, 1955
This is the first volume in *The Pelican History of England*. It provides a clear and sound background for a teacher who wants to be historically accurate while teaching from this book. There is a good bibliography at the back for further reading.

Roman London
A. Sorrell, Batsford, 1969
This is an excellent book and should be on the library shelves. The text is clear and concise, and Mr Sorrell's drawings of Londinium are large, bold and exciting, catching the atmosphere brilliantly. A great deal of further imaginative work might well develop from this book.

The Roman Imperial Army
G. Webster, Black, 1968
Apart from the extensive and scholarly text, which may well be of

interest to teachers, this book is very well illustrated with photo-graphs, and many of the excellent line drawings could be the basis for wall-charts.

5   Fiction of Roman Britain for pupils

With few exceptions, the books used in the body of this volume are suitable for pupils. In addition, the following are worth reading.

Twilight Province
G. Finkel, Angus & Robertson, 1967
This book is set in the Durham area about AD 520. The Roman occupation is over, and those who have stayed behind join with the Picts against the heathen invaders. The book tells of the adventures of the son of a local Roman 'king' in this northern part of Britain.

The Eastern Beacon
M. Ray, Jonathan Cape, 1965
A young Greek girl and a Roman boy are shipwrecked on the Scilly Isles in AD 296 and become the slaves of the natives there. The book is a sensitive account of their life as they tend the beacon which is to give warning against attack by pirates—or Romans.

Spring Tide
M. Ray, Faber, 1969
Christians are being persecuted in Britain when two young Romans find that a man they know is a priest of the hunted religion.

The Eagle of the Ninth
R. Sutcliff, Oxford, 1955
A young Roman soldier tries to find the lost battle-standard of the vanished Ninth Legion in Caledonia. This is only one of the books on Roman Britain by Miss Sutcliff, an outstanding writer of historical fiction.

Outcast
R. Sutcliff, Oxford, 1955
This book tells of a young Roman who becomes the leader of a British tribe. He is an outcast, and much of the book is concerned with his harsh life before he finally finds a strange happiness.

The Silver Branch
R. Sutcliff, Oxford, 1957
This book is the tale of two young Romans who help to overthrow a usurping Emperor. Apart from its excitement, the book is valuable as one of the few written about the later years of Roman Britain.

The Bronze Sword
H. Treece, Hamish Hamilton (Antelope Book), 1969
This is a brief and simple tale about a retired centurion whose peaceful way of life is shattered by Boudicca's rebellion.